Ramen

for Beginners

**Make Traditional Healthy and Delicious
Ramen Recipes in Your Home**

Hikaru Tawara

TABLE OF CONTENT

Introduction   **4**

Ramen Recipes   **5**

INTRODUCTION

Ramen consists mostly of broth and noodles. On the surface, it appears to be a fairly straightforward dish, but when cooked by masters, it reveals a wealth of nuance, skill, and tremendous depths of flavor that belie its apparent simplicity. Ramen, for instance, may take on countless forms, based on factors such as the soup base, noodles used, toppings, and additional sides.

In Japanese cuisine, shio (salt), miso (soybean paste), shoyu (soy sauce), and tonkotsu (pork bone broth) are the most often used bases (pork bone). Although the meat used in shoyu and shio varies by area, it is often chicken broth. Hokkaido, in the north, is where miso was first created, whereas Kyushu is where tonkotsu is often consumed.

Most restaurants serving Japanese ramen will let you specify the thickness and "doneness" of your noodles. For instance, they can be cooked until thick, thin, or normal, and then either regular or hard. One's own tastes will determine the answer.

The last component of ramen is the toppings, which vary greatly not only by location but also by establishment. Thin slices of braised or roasted pork called chashu are a popular topping for ramen, as are eggs cooked in a variety of ways (hard boiled, soft boiled, poached, and even raw), as well as scallions, bamboo, dried seaweed, steamed fish cake, canned corn, and pats of butter. Typically, chopsticks are used to consume the food, and a Chinese soup spoon is used to scoop up the broth.

RAMEN RECIPES

CHICKPEA RAMEN SOUP

Prep time: 15 minutes

Total time: 40 minutes

Serving:6

Ingredients

- 2 tbsp of extra-virgin olive oil
- 1 medium yellow onion, chopped
- 1 cup of thinly sliced celery
- 1 cup of carrots, peeled and cut
- ¼ tsp of salt, more as need
- ½ tsp of ground turmeric
- ½ tsp of curry powder
- 1 bay leaf
- 1 can chickpeas, rinsed and drained
- 8 oz. of spiral pasta
- 2 tbsp of chopped fresh flat-leaf parsley
- 2 quarts vegetable broth
- Freshly ground black pepper, as need

Instructions

1. Olive oil should be warmed in a large soup pot or Dutch oven over medium heat. The onion, celery, and carrots should be added to the oil once it has reveryed a shimmer and a quarter of a tsp of of salt has been dispersed throughout. In a medium saucepan over medium heat, cook the onions, stirring often, for 5–7 minutes, or until they become translucent and tender.

2. To bring out their full flavors, add the turmeric and curry powder (if using) and stir continually for about 30 seconds. Throw in some chickpeas, some pasta, some parsley, and some broth, and a bay leaf.
3. Bring the sauce to a boil over high heat, then lower to a simmer over medium heat and cook until the pasta is al dente, 10 to 20 minutes.
4. Take the saucepan off the heat and pepper it heavily. You may want to season it with additional salt if you think it's missing anything. Serve immediately while still hot, and sprinkle with more parsley and pepper if desired.
5. Once the soup has cooled, cover it and keep it in the fridge for up to five days.

CHICKEN VEGETABLE RAMEN NOODLES

Prep time: 10 minutes

Total time: 18 minutes

Serving: 3

Ingredients

- 2 packets ramen instant noodles
- 1 tbsp of oil
- 2 garlic cloves, minced
- 1/2 onion, sliced
- 200g chicken thighs, cut into bite size pieces
- 1 1/4 cups of water, + more as needed
- 1 carrot, cut into matchsticks
- 1 small red capsicum
- 2 cups of cabbage, finely sliced

Sauce:

- 1 tbsp of dark soy sauce
- 1 tbsp of Oyster sauce
- 2 tsp of Hoisin sauce
- 1 tbsp of Mirin

Garnishes (optional):

- Finely sliced green onion

Instructions

1. Combining the Sauce.
2. Put the oil in a big pan and heat it over high heat. Cook the onion and garlic for about 1 minute and a half, or until they begin to turn golden.
3. Toss in the chicken and cook just until the outside is mostly white.
4. As soon as the chicken begins to turn a deep golden color, add the sauce and continue cooking for another minute.
5. Cook the carrots and peppers for a minute after adding them.
6. Remove some of the chicken and vegetables to create room for the noodles. To the boiling water, add the noodles.
7. Wait 45 seconds until the water's edge begins to boil before turning the noodles.
8. Wait 30 seconds, then stir in the chicken and vegetables after untangling the noodles.
9. Once the noodles are done and the sauce has reduced enough to coat them, add the cabbage and mix for one minute.
10. Green onions are optional but highly recommended as a last-minute garnish.

GINGER GARLIC CHICKEN RAMEN

Prep time: 15 minutes

Total time: 1 hours 15 minutes

Serving: 8

Ingredients

- 8 c. chicken stock
- 1 1/2 lb. of boneless, skinless chicken breast
- 1piece fresh ginger, halved lengthwise
- 6 garlic cloves, sliced
- 1 package shiitake mushrooms, halved
- 1 tbsp of. soy sauce
- 2 tsp of. toasted sesame oil
- 3 packages dried ramen
- 4 baby bok choy, separated into leaves
- 2 c. snow peas
- 3 scallions, sliced

Directions

1. Add chicken, ginger, garlic, and stock to a large saucepan or Dutch oven. Coax into a boil by increasing the heat. Cover and boil over low heat until chicken is fully cooked, about 25-30 minutes. After 8-10 minutes of simmering with the lid on, the mushrooms should be delicate enough to eat. With two forks, shred the chicken once it has been removed.
2. Add the noodles to the saucepan and simmer, stirring periodically, for 2 to 4 minutes, or until they begin to soften. Add the chicken, bok choy, and snow peas and stir well. Steam for 1-2 minutes, or until veggies are bright green and soft. Incorporate the scallions right before serving.

10 MINUTES TANTANMEN RAMEN

Prep time: 5 minutes

Total time: 10 minutes

Serving: 2

Ingredients

For Tare (Seasoning Sauce)

- 3 tbsp of Tsuyu, Japanese soup base sauce
- 2 tbsp of tahini
- 1 tbsp of chili oil

For Meat

- 2 tbsp of chili oil or regular cooking oil
- 3 cloves garlic, chopped
- 1 oz ginger, chopped
- 1 tbsp of toban djan, Chinese chili bean paste
- 1 tbsp of oyster sauce
- 1/2 lb ground pork, beef, chicken
- 3 tbsp of rice wine

For Soup

- 1 cup of water
- 2 cups of un-sweetened soy
- 2 tsp of chicken powder

For Noodles & Toppings

- 1 baby bok choy, cut
- handful beansprouts
- 2 portions fresh, frozen
- 1 to 2 green onions, chopped
- 1 ramen egg, cut into half

- sesame seeds & sansyo powder

Instructions

1. Put in the tare ingredients and mix thoroughly with a whisk. Remove from consideration.
2. Water, soy milk, and chicken powder should be mixd in a medium-sized saucepan. Bring it to a gentle simmer, covered. Keep an eye on it because it can easily explode if left alone. Do something same with another pot of water, and get it boiling.
3. Put the chile oil, garlic, and ginger in a big wok and cook it up over high heat. Just until the scent is released, around 30 seconds, stir in the toban djan and oyster sauce. Add ground pork to the pan and continue to stir-fry for another 45 seconds to 1 minute. Stir fry the pork for roughly a minute with the sauce once you've broken it up. Stir-fry the pork for three to four minutes in rice wine until the liquid has evaporated and the meat is thoroughly done. Take off the burner and keep warm.
4. Bok choy should be blanched in boiling salted water for 1 minute. Discard the water and set the noodles aside. Bean sprouts, a handful's worth, should be added to the boiling water and left to cook for 2 minutes. Discard the water and set the noodles aside.
5. Place the noodles in the pot of boiling water after it has stopped boiling, and cook them in accordance with the package's instructions. If using fresh or frozen noodles, prepare only one serving at a time. While the noodles are boiling (fresh or frozen, 1–2 minutes), mix the tare with half of the hot broth in a serving dish.
6. Cooked noodles should be drained (the additional liquid will dilute the broth and tastes) and added to the dish. Organize the noodles and stir them in the liquid so that they are all uniformly coated. Bean sprouts, bok choy, pork, chile oil as

need, a ramen egg, green onions, sesame seeds, and sansyo powder make excellent toppings for ramen.

EASY CHICKEN AND VEGETABLE RAMEN

Prep time: 20 minutes

Total time: 2 hours 50 minutes

Serving: 4

Ingredients

Chicken Stock:

- 2½ lb. of whole chicken cut up
- 6 cups of water
- 1 yellow onion peeled and quartered
- 1 head garlic halved cross-wise
- 1 inch piece of ginger cut
- 2 tsp of sesame oil
- 3 tbsp of soy sauce
- Salt and pepper as need

Ramen:

- 2 tsp of neutral cooking oil
- 1 shallot peeled and diced
- 8 oz. of mushrooms trimmed and sliced
- 1 red chili pepper trimmed and sliced into rounds
- 2 tsp of mirin
- 1 head bok choy washed
- 1 tbsp of white miso paste
- 16 oz. of fresh ramen
- 2 radishes thinly sliced, optional, for garnish
- Chili oil optional, for garnish

- Salt and pepper as need

Instructions

Cook the Chicken Stock:

1. In a big saucepan, submerge the chicken in at least 6 cups of of water (more if necessary). Soy sauce, sesame oil, onion, garlic, and ginger should be added. Add a lot of salt as need. Put over high heat until it boils. If you want the chicken to fall off the bone and the broth to darken and reduce to no more than 3 cups of, lower the heat and let it simmer, uncovered, for at least an hour.

Strain the Stock:

2. Put the garlic and chicken in a basin. Put the stock through a fine mesh sieve into a big basin; then, dispose of the sediments. Clean the pan and put it back on the burner.

Finish the Stock:

3. Remove the meat from the bird and discard the bones. Remove the garlic cloves and mash the garlic cloves gently into the chicken. Get rid of the garlic's papery peel. If you want to preserve the chicken and garlic from drying out, you may put the dish of them in the stock.

Finish the Ramen:

4. Over medium heat, warm the neutral oil in the same big pot used for the stock. Cook the shallot and mushrooms for 6-8 minutes, or until the mushrooms start to brown. Toss in the chili pepper and heat for a minute, or until aromatic.
5. Add 3 cups of of water and the chicken stock, then pour in the chicken. Then, while it's boiling, sprinkle on some mirin. You may always season as need by adding extra soy sauce or sesame oil. In order to avoid a salty soup, please refrain from adding too much salt to the stock. Turn the heat down and

simmer uncovered for 15 minutes. You can always add more seasoning after a taste test.

6. Cook the bok choy in the broth for about 7 minutes, or until it has turned a vibrant green color. As soon as the heat is turned off, whisk in the miso paste.

Cook the Ramen:

1. Boil the ramen in water according to the package directions while the soup finishes simmering. After it has been cooked, drain the ramen and serve it in four separate bowls.
2. Pour the ramen soup over the noodles and top with sliced radishes and chile oil. Enjoy!

PULLED PORK RAMEN

Prep time: 20 minutes

Total time: 1 day 12 hours 50 minutes

Serving: 2

Ingredients

Ramen Broth:

- 2 lb. of chicken bones
- 4 oz. of kombu
- 4 oz. of dried shittake mushrooms
- 2 oz. of fresh ginger
- 2 oz. of soy sauce
- 2 oz. of rice wine vinegar
- 1 oz. of bonito flakes
- 4 scallions
- 2 carrots
- 2 celery stalks

- 2 cloves garlic
- 2 tomatoes
- 1/2 lemon
- 1/2 pig foot

Braised pork butt:

- Salt and pepper
- 1 1/2 lb. of pork butt
- Olive oil, for cooking
- 12 oz. of chicken stock
- 2 oz. of fresh ginger
- 2 bay leaves
- 2 celery stalks
- 2 cloves garlic
- 2 tomatoes
- 1 onion

Ramen:

- 6 oz. of ramen noodles
- Salt
- 1 oz. of pureed pork lard
- 2 oz. of cooked pork belly, warm
- 2 oz. of bamboo shoots
- 1 oz. of fresh arugula
- 1 oz. of fresh spinach
- 1/2 hard-boiled egg, optional
- 1 oz. of diced green onions

Directions

1. Place the chicken bones, kombu, mushrooms, ginger, soy sauce, vinegar, bonito flakes, scallions, carrots, celery, garlic, tomatoes, lemon, and pig foot in a large stock pot. Bring the pot of water to a boil, then reduce the heat and let it simmer for about 36 hours. Remove any chunks by straining.

2. In order to braise the pork butt, set the oven temperature to 350 degrees F.
3. Season the pork butt generously with salt and pepper, then sear it in olive oil over high heat until it's browned all over. Add the stock, ginger, bay leaves, celery, garlic, tomatoes, and onion to a baking dish and bake for 2 hours 30 minutes to 3 hours.
4. Ramen noodles should be cooked in lightly salted boiling water for 4–6 minutes, depending on how soft you like them. Warm up a saucepan with 12 oz. of broth. Pour boiling broth over fat and noodles, and serve immediately. Add bamboo shoots and top with pork belly and 4 oz. of pig butt. Add some arugula and spinach on top. A hard-boiled egg and some green onions are a nice addition.

CHICKEN MARSALA PASTA

Prep time: 10 minutes

Total time: 30 minutes

Serving: 4

Ingredients

- 8 oz. of uncooked pasta
- 1 tbsp of olive oil
- 2 tbsp of butter divided
- 2 large chicken breasts cut into small pieces
- 1/4 tsp of garlic powder
- Flour for dredging
- 8 oz. of cremini mushrooms
- 1/2 cup of marsala wine
- 1/2 cup of chicken broth
- 1/2 tsp of Dijon mustard

- 1/2 cup of heavy/whipping cream
- Salt & pepper as need
- Freshly grated parmesan cheese as need

Instructions

1. To cook the pasta, bring a big pot of salted water to a boil. Pasta should be cooked to the al dente texture specified by the box.
2. The chicken should be cut into small pieces, dusted with garlic powder, then dredged in flour.
3. Over medium heat, put the olive oil and 1 tbsp of the butter in a pan.
4. Add the chicken to a heated skillet. Allow it to cook for 5–6 minutes, tossing periodically, until the chicken is gently browned. Remove the chicken from the heat and put it to one side.
5. Coat the pan with the remaining butter. During this time, add the mushrooms and simmer for another 3–4 minutes, or until the water they've emitted has been boiled down. The mushrooms should be removed from the heat (ok to put on same plate as chicken).
6. Throw in some chicken stock, some marsala, and some Dijon mustard. Give it a good stir until the mustard is completely dissolved, then let it boil for about two minutes.
7. Reduce the heat to medium and add the cream, chicken, and mushrooms to the pan. Continue cooking for a few more minutes, or until the chicken is fully cooked and the sauce has thickened.
8. Put salt and pepper on it if it needs it. Cook the pasta according to the package directions, then drain it and mix it with the sauce (thinning the sauce with some of the pasta water if necessary).

30 MINUTE CURRY RAMEN

Prep time: 10 minutes

Total time: 15 minutes

Serving: 2

Ingredients

- 8 oz top sirloin
- 4 cups of low or no sodium chicken broth
- 2 large eggs
- 2 cubes Japanese curry
- ramen noodles
- a bit of oil
- green onion to garnish

Instructions

1. Noodles require a pot of boiling water, so prepare that now.
2. Prepare the meat or poultry for cooking.
3. Cut the meat into thin strips, or the chicken into cubes about 3/4 inches on a side.
4. A pan big enough to accommodate the stock should be heated until the oil shimmers.
5. Brown the meat in a skillet until it reveryes an internal temperature of 165 degrees. Remove.
6. Eggs cooked to a medium degree
7. The eggs should be cooked for 6 1/2 minutes in the water used to prepare the noodles, which should be brought to a boil.
8. After 6 1/2 minutes, transfer the eggs to cold water to stop the cooking process. It's important that they cool rapidly so that the yolks don't solidify.

9. After waiting for the eggs to cool, cut them in half lengthwise. Always use caution. The egg yolks are still a little runny in texture.

Make the broth

1. Cut the cubes into little pieces.
2. Apply some chicken stock to deglaze the pan, then add another cup of or so.
3. Throw the cubed meat into the stock and get it boiling. You'll need a spatula to hunt these things down because they don't dissolve very quickly.
4. When the cubes are dissolved, pour in the remaining liquid and keep cooking for another four to five minutes.
5. While the stock is warming, prepare the ramen noodles according to the package's directions.
6. We recommend draining the noodles.

To serve

1. Split the ramen between two plates. Place the meat of your choice on the noodles, and then ladle half of the soup into every serving bowl. To gently reheat the eggs, add them and submerge them.
2. Sprinkle some chopped green onion on top, then dig it!

EASY GINGER CHICKEN AND SPINACH RAMEN

Prep time: 15 minutes

Total time: 15 minutes

Serving: 4

Ingredients

- 3/4 lb. of boneless skinless chicken breasts
- 4 cups of low sodium chicken broth
- 1/3 cup of low sodium soy sauce
- 1/4 cup of red curry paste
- 1 oz. of dried porcini mushrooms
- 1 tbsp of fresh grated ginger
- 1 tbsp of Chinese 5 spice
- 1 tsp of black pepper
- 2 tsp of honey
- 3/4 cup of canned coconut milk
- 4 squares ramen noodles
- 3 cups of baby spinach
- 1 acorn squash – cubed, or 3 cups of cubed butternut squash
- 1 tbsp of extra-virgin olive oil
- 1 tbsp of spicy curry powder
- kosher salt and black pepper
- soft- or hard-boiled eggs, for serving
- carrots, green onions, chilies, and cilantro, for serving

Instructions

Crockpot

1. chicken broth, 4 cups of water, Chicken, soy sauce, dried mushrooms, ginger, curry paste, Chinese 5 spice, pepper, and honey should all be mixed together in the crock pot's bowl.

Keep covered and cook for 4-6 hours on low or 2-4 hours on high.

2. Set the oven to 425 degrees Fahrenheit before serving. Mix the squash, olive oil, curry powder, salt, and pepper on a baking sheet and toss to coat. Roast for 25 to 30 minutes, or until soft.

3. Turn the crockpot up to high. Separate the chicken into shreds. Toss the spinach and coconut milk together. The noodles should be well immersed in the soup. Soak for 8-10 minutes, or until noodles are pliable.

4. Divide the soup into bowls, and sprinkle every serving with roasted squash and any additional toppings you choose. Enjoy!

Instant pot

1. Turn the oven temperature up to 425 degrees Fahrenheit.

2. Chicken, chicken broth, 4 cups of water, soy sauce, curry paste, dried mushrooms, ginger, Chinese 5 spice, pepper, and honey should all be mixd in the instant pot's bowl and stirred thoroughly before cooking. Cook for 8 minutes with the lid on.

3. Mix the squash, olive oil, curry powder, salt, and pepper on a baking sheet. Cook for 25 to 30 minutes, or until soft.

4. Turn the instant pot to the sauté setting and release the steam. You should shred the chicken. Put the spinach and coconut milk in a pot and stir. Next, place noodles in the liquid. Set aside for 5 minutes to allow noodles to soften.

5. To serve, spoon the soup into bowls and top with the roasted squash and any additional ingredients you want. Enjoy!

Stove

1. Turn the oven temperature up to 425 degrees Fahrenheit.

2. The chicken, 4 cups of water, soy sauce, curry paste, dried mushrooms, ginger, chicken broth, pepper, Chinese 5 spice, and honey should all be mixd in a big soup pot and stirred

thoroughly. Bring to a boil over medium heat, then lower the heat to maintain a gentle simmer for 15 minutes, or until the chicken is cooked through and easily shredded.

3. Mix the squash, olive oil, curry powder, salt, and pepper on a baking sheet. Cook for 25 to 30 minutes, or until soft.
4. When the chicken is done cooking, shred it. Over high heat, bring the soup to a boil. Put the spinach and coconut milk in a pot and stir. Next, place noodles in the liquid. Noodles should be soft after three to five minutes of cooking time.
5. Sprinkle peanuts and toasted sesame oil over the soup before serving. Enjoy!

VEGETARIAN GREEN CURRY RAMEN

Prep time: 20 minutes

Total time: 50 minutes

Serving: 2

Ingredients

- 2 Tbsp of Cooking Oil
- 8 oz. of Shiitake Mushrooms, sliced
- 1 Tbsp of Low Sodium Soy Sauce
- 2 cloves Garlic, minced
- 1 ¾ cup of Coconut Milk, divided
- 3 Tbsp of Thai Green Curry Paste
- 3 cups of Vegetable Stock
- 1 Tbsp of Brown Sugar
- 1 ½ Tbsp of Fish Sauce
- 1 packet Instant Ramen Noodles
- 5 oz. of Baby Spinach
- 1 cup of Shelled Edamame
- Green Onions, thinly sliced

- Sesame Seeds, white or black, for serving
- Sriracha, for serving

Instructions

1. Start boiling a small saucepan of water for the eggs.
2. While the water is heating up, get the oil ready in a big, heavy-bottomed saucepan or wok.
3. When the oil is heated, add the shiitake mushrooms and sauté them for 5 to 7 minutes, or until they are a deep golden brown. Cook the mushrooms in the soy sauce and garlic until the soy sauce has been absorbed. Put aside for a moment.
4. Green curry paste and 2 tbsp of of coconut milk can be added to a hot pot. Fry for about 2 minutes, or until the aroma is released.
5. Mix in the remaining coconut milk, the rest of the brown sugar, the fish sauce, and the vegetable stock. Do not boil, but simmer.
6. Add ramen noodles to the broth after it has come to a boil. Don't overcook the ramen; it should be soft when done (follow the cooking instructions on the box).
7. Meanwhile, put the eggs back into the saucepan and lower the heat down to a simmer. Drop eggs into water that is just simmering. If the eggs are at room temperature, simmer for 7 minutes; if they've been in the fridge, simmer for 8 minutes.
8. After the spinach has wilted, remove the ramen from the heat and mix in the edamame.
9. Separate the ramen and broth into several big dishes. Place a few mushrooms on every serving.
10. Prepare eggs by peeling and halving them. Set eggs on the ramen. Top with scallions, sesame seeds, and Sriracha sauce for more heat.

CHICKEN RAMEN NOODLE DUMP DINNER

Prep time: 15 minutes

Total time: 45 minutes

Serving: 8

Ingredients

- Six 3-oz. of packages chicken-flavored instant ramen noodles
- One 8-oz. of container scallion cream cheese
- 4 cups of whole milk
- 2 cups of shredded rotisserie chicken
- One 10.8-oz. of bag frozen broccoli florets
- 8 oz. of shredded Cheddar

Directions

1. The oven has to be preheated to 400 degrees F.
2. Line the bottom of a 13-by-9-inch baking dish with the ramen squares. In a medium bowl, mix the cream cheese, milk, and the one ramen flavor packet you set aside, whisking to mix. The ramen is served with the sauce. Put the chicken and broccoli on top of the noodles and sauce and spread them out. Spread the Cheddar cheese over the top of the dish in an equal layer.
3. Pasta should be fully cooked after 30–35 minutes in the oven, while cream sauce should be bubbling and cheese should have melted.

EXPRESS BUTTER CORN & PORK MISO RAMEN

Prep time: 15 minutes

Total time: 30 minutes

Serving: 4

Ingredients

- 800g cooked ramen noodles
- 2 tbsp of butter
- 1½ cups of frozen corn kernels
- 8 cups of chicken stock
- 2 soy sauce eggs
- ½ cup of finely sliced cabbage
- ¼ cup of finely sliced spring onion
- sesame seeds

Miso tare:

- ¾ cup of mirin
- 1 garlic cloves, finely grated
- 2 tsp of finely grated ginger
- ¼ cup of shiro miso paste

Pork topping:

- 1 tbsp of vegetable oil
- 4 garlic cloves, finely chopped
- 250g (8.8 oz) pork mince
- 2 tbsp of soy sauce

Directions

1. Cook the mirin, garlic, and ginger in a small saucepan over medium heat to make the tare. Miso should be dissolved into a beverage at a low simmer. put off for later use.

2. Put the oil in a frying pan and set it over high heat to prepare the pork topping. Stir-fry the pork and garlic for two to three minutes, or until the meat is nearly done. Cook the pork in the soy sauce until the liquid has disappeared and the meat is no longer pink in the middle. Take away from the heat and put in a cool place.
3. Melt the butter in a medium-high oven in the same pan you used to cook the pork. Stir in the corn and cook for a few minutes until it is hot.
4. Serve the ramen noodles in individual dishes.
5. Chicken stock should be heated in a big pot over high heat. Stir in the miso tare and keep cooking until the sauce thickens. Spoon the broth over the noodles. Layer the pork, corn, and a sliver of chopped cabbage on top. Add more butter on top of the corn. Toss in a halved egg, some spring onion, and some sesame seeds for garnish.

RAMEN WITH SESAME GINGER MEATBALLS

Prep time: 1hours

Total time: 1 hours 30 minutes

Serving: 4

Ingredients

Meatballs

- 1 lb. of ground chicken
- 1/2 cup of plain bread crumbs
- 3 scallions minced
- 3 tbsp of minced fresh ginger
- 2 garlic cloves minced
- 1 large egg beaten
- 2 tsp of sesame oil

- 2 tsp of low sodium soy sauce or tamari
- 2 tsp of Sriracha or chili paste
- 1/4 tsp of salt

Ramen Noodles and Broth

- 6 cups of low sodium chicken stock
- 1 tsp of fresh minced ginger
- 2 garlic cloves minced
- 2 tsp of low sodium soy sauce or tamari
- 1 cup of shredded carrots
- 1 cup of bok choy chopped
- 8 oz. of Plain, unseasoned ramen noodles
- salt as need
- 1/4 cup of chopped cilantro
- 1/4 cup of chopped scallions
- Sriracha serving

Instructions

To make the meatballs:

1. It's time to heat up the oven to 450 degrees. Line Two parchment-lined baking sheets for convenience.
2. All the meatball components should be mixed together in one big dish. Do not overmix; use a spatula or your hands to blend ingredients.
3. Make meatballs approximately an inch in diameter by scooping out about 1 tbsp of of the mixture using a cookie scoop or small spoon. Make sure the meatballs are evenly spread out on both baking pans. Depending on their size, you should get roughly 20 meatballs.
4. Prepare meatballs for oven cooking for 12-15 minutes. Brown all sides by flipping them over halfway through cooking.

To make the broth:

1. While the meatballs are roasting, make the sauce by combining the stock, ginger, garlic, and soy sauce or tamari in a large skillet or Dutch oven. Get the ingredients boiling, then turn the heat down to medium.
2. Mix in the shredded carrots, bok choy, noodles, and a pinch of salt. Cover and simmer for approximately 10 minutes, or until the veggies are tender. They will taste much better if you don't cook them too long.
3. If you want your cilantro and scallions to maintain their crunch, add them right before serving.
4. Add a couple meatballs and some additional Sriracha or chilli sauce to your bowl of ramen and serve.

CHICKEN DIABLO

Prep time: 15minutes

Total time: 2 hours 30 minutes

Serving: 4

Ingredients

- ½ cup of hot pepper sauce
- 1 cup of reduced fat sour cream
- ½ cup of ketchup
- ¼ cup of honey
- ¼ tsp of paprika
- ¼ tsp of cumin
- 8 skinless, boneless chicken breast halves
- ¼ cup of vegetable oil
- 2 cloves garlic, minced

Directions

1. Pepper sauce, sour cream, ketchup, and honey should all be mixd in a medium bowl and stirred until smooth. Add paprika and cumin for flavor. Save half the sauce for serving later, and use the rest to marinade some chicken breasts. Refrigerate for at least two hours after covering.
2. Prepare a big amount of vegetable oil in a pan over medium heat. Cook the garlic until the aroma is released. Toss marinated chicken breasts into the pan and cook for 20 minutes, turning once, or until golden brown and cooked through.
3. Meanwhile, in a small saucepan, bring the remaining marinade to a boil and let it simmer for 3–5 minutes.
4. Serve chicken breasts on a bed of warm sauce.

HOLLANDAISE-TOPPED PARMESAN CHICKEN

Prep time: 15minutes

Total time: 40 minutes

Serving: 4

Ingredients

- 1 cup of crushed round buttery crackers
- ¼ cup of shredded Parmesan cheese
- ¼ tsp of garlic powder
- ¼ cup of butter, melted
- ¾ lb boneless, skinless chicken breasts
- ½ (1.6-oz) pkg hollandaise sauce mix

Instructions

1. Set oven temperature to 350 degrees F. In a small bowl, mix the cracker crumbs, cheese, and garlic powder. Separate a small basin for the melted butter.

2. Chicken breasts should be halved lengthwise, and then lb. to a thickness of half an inch in a plastic bag sealed at one end with the heel of your hand or a meat mallet. Just a little of salt and pepper will do.
3. Coat chicken with cracker mixture, then dip in melted butter. Arrange on a rimmed baking sheet and drizzle with the remaining butter.
4. Put the chicken in an uncovered baking dish and bake for about 25-30 minutes.
5. Follow the directions on the hollandaise sauce packet and use it to top the chicken.

BIRRIA RAMEN

Prep time: 20 minutes

Total time: 3 hours 50 minutes

Serving: 8

Ingredients

- 7-8 cups of water
- 4 lb. of chuck roast, cut
- 2 lb. of short ribs
- 1 large white onion, dry skins removed, cut
- 1 garlic bulb, cut
- 1 carrot , cut
- 5 bay leaves, dried
- 8 guajillo chiles, stems cut
- 3 tbsp of chicken bouillon
- 1-2 tsp of chili powder
- 1 tsp of mexican oregano
- 1 tsp of ground cumin
- 1 tsp of salt, adjust as need

- 4 ramen noodles

Toppings

- radishes, sliced
- cabbage, shredded
- cilantro, diced
- white onion, diced

Instructions

1. Put the meat, onion, garlic, carrot, and dried peppers in a big saucepan. Put water on top of it.
2. Season with Chicken Bouillon, Oregano, Cumin, and Salt and bring to a boil, stirring occasionally. Get the water boiling. Then lower the heat and keep simmering.
3. After 30 minutes, skim the surface of the pot to remove any floaties that have risen to the top during the bone's cooking out.
4. Peppers may be blended by removing the softened skins and placing them in a blender or food processor. As required, add up to a quarter cup of broth and blend again until smooth.
5. Peppers: If there are any shreds of skin that need to be removed, strain the peppers.
6. Cook the peppers in a blender and then add them to the broth.
7. Modify Flavorings by Adding Chili Powder as need to Turn the Broth a Rich Red.
8. Simmer, covered, for at least three hours, or until the meat can be easily shredded with two forks. Take the cover off every 40 minutes or so and give it a good stir. Once the meat is done, you may also adjust the seasoning by tasting the broth and making any necessary adjustments.
9. Remove the fat that has risen to the surface of the soup by skimming.

10. Toss out the aromatics: the broth's onion, garlic, carrots, and bay leaves.
11. Scoop the meat out of the soup and shred it. Discard any skeletons.

20-MINUTE SKILLET MUSHROOM CHICKEN

Prep time: 10 minutes

Total time: 20 minutes

Serving: 5

Ingredients

For Chicken

- 1 ½ lb boneless skinless chicken breasts
- Kosher salt and black pepper
- 1 tsp of oregano
- 1 tsp of paprika
- 1 tsp of coriander
- 2 tbsp of extra virgin olive oil

For Mushroom Sauce

- 1 tbsp of ghee or unsalted butter
- 12 oz. of fresh large mushrooms, sliced
- ½ cup of chicken broth
- 3 green onions, chopped
- 2 garlic cloves, minced
- kosher salt and black pepper
- Parsley for garnish

Instructions

1. Bake at 200 degrees Fahrenheit. You'll need it to maintain the chicken at a comfortable temperature.
2. Chicken cutlets may be made by slicing a whole chicken breast in half horizontally. Season with salt and pepper after drying. Put some oregano, paprika, and coriander in a bowl and mix them together. Spread the spice mixture on both sides of the chicken.
3. A big pan with 2 tbsp of of extra virgin olive oil should be heated until shimmering but not smoking. Toss in the chicken cutlets and cook for about 3 minutes on one side before flipping. Cut into a slice with a small, sharp knife to see if the inside is cooked. Put the chicken on a baking sheet or other oven-safe dish and bake it.
4. Put just a touch more extra virgin olive oil into the same pan. Melt some ghee and add it to the mix. The mushrooms need about 5 minutes in a saute pan. Soup base, scallions, garlic, salt, and pepper should be added. Get the water boiling.
5. Return the chicken to the pan and drizzle some of the sauce over it. Don't wait around; serve right away.

HOME-MADE RAMEN BROTH

Prep time: 25 minutes

Total time: 2 hours 55 minutes

Serving: 4

Ingredients

Ramen Broth

- 2.2-2.6lb chicken carcasses
- 2.2lb pork soup bones
- 1 onion , peeled
- 3 green onions green part only

- 3cm cube ginger , cut in half
- 2 cloves garlic
- 10g bonito flakes in a spice bag
- Shōyu Ramen Broth
- 2 tbsp of konbu soy sauce
- 1½ tsp of mirin
- salt to adjust flavour
- 10-13.5oz Ramen Broth in this recipe , boiling hot

Shōyu Ramen Noodles and Toppings

- 80-100g/2.8-3.5oz fresh thin egg noodles
- 2-3 slices Yakibuta
- 1 Ramen Egg
- 2 tbsp of shiraga negi finely julienned green onion
- 1 10cm2/4"2 yakinori

Instructions

Ramen Broth

1. In a saucepan, bring 4 liters (or 8.5 cups of) of water to a boil. Boil the chicken and pig bones for 10 minutes. Many low-lifes will emerge.
2. One by one, rinse the bones in cold running water to get rid of the coagulated blood, the chicken's intestines along the spine, and the other brown, grimy parts.
3. Bring 4 liters (8.5 cups of) of water to a boil in a big saucepan, then add the cleaned bones and the remaining Ramen Broth ingredients (except for the bonito flakes).
4. Scum may be removed by using a ladle to gently remove it when it rises to the surface (note 5). When skimming off the scum, don't stir the liquid with the ladle since it will make the broth hazy.
5. Once the scum has been removed four to five times, reduce the heat to a low simmer.
6. At the outset of simmering, skim off any scum that forms.

7. Simmer, covered but with vents slightly ajar, for 2 hours. Then sprinkle in a package of bonito flakes. Reduce heat and simmer for a few minutes.
8. Stop using heat if it's not necessary. To extract the liquid, strain the soup with a strainer.
9. Yields roughly 3.4 cups of (1.6 liters) of soup.

Making Shōyu Ramen

1. Mix the mirin and konbu soy sauce in a serving dish.
2. Put a pot of water on to boil, add the noodles, and then drain them well.
3. Stir in the Ramen broth until everything is well mixd. Add salt as need after testing the soup.
4. Stir in the noodles. Slide a sheet of yaki nori up the edge of the bowl and top it with sliced Yakibuta, Ramen Eggs, and shraga negi. Don't wait around; serve right away.

RAMEN CARBONARA

Prep time: 5 minutes

Total time: 15 minutes

Serving: 4

Ingredients

- 9 oz. of ramen noodles
- 1 tbsp of olive oil
- 8 slices bacon
- 3 cloves garlic
- 2 large eggs
- 1 cup of Parmesan cheese
- ¼ tsp of salt
- ¼ tsp of pepper

- 4 tbsp of basil

Instructions

1. Prepare the noodles by following the package directions for cooking ramen. Time spent cooking them shouldn't exceed a few minutes. To prevent them from sticking together, toss them with the olive oil.
2. To make the egg mixture, put the eggs and Parmesan cheese in a medium basin and whisk until mixd. Keep out of the way for the time being.
3. Bacon should be cooked in a big pan until it is golden and crispy. Remove excess fat from the pan, but save 1 tbsp of of bacon grease. Sauté the garlic for 30 seconds, or until it begins to release its scent.
4. To complete the carbonara, mix the ramen noodles with the bacon in a pan. Take it off the stove immediately. Mix the eggs and cheese and pour over the noodles, tossing to coat. Egg will be cooked to preference by the piping hot noodles.
5. Serve immediately while still hot, and top with finely chopped basil and additional freshly ground black pepper for garnish.

SPICY PORK THAI COCONUT CURRY RAMEN

Prep time: 15 minutes

Total time: 45 minutes

Serving: 4

Ingredients

- 2 tbsp of sambal oelek
- 2 shallots, halved
- 6 cloves garlic

- 1 (2 inch) piece ginger, peeled and sliced
- 1/4 cup of cilantro stems, chopped
- 1 tbsp of ground coriander
- 1 tbsp of ground turmeric
- 1 tsp of curry powder
- 1 tbsp of vegetable or canola oil
- 2 cans unsweetened coconut milk
- 2 cups of chicken broth
- 1 tbsp of fish sauce
- 1 tbsp of light brown sugar
- Kosher salt
- Spicy Pork
- 4 packages instant ramen noodles, flavor packets discarded
- 4 eggs
- 1 bunch scallions, chopped
- 1 lime, sliced into wedges
- Cilantro, for garnish

For the spicy pork

- 1 tbsp of vegetable or canola oil
- 1 lb. of ground pork
- 2–3 tsp of sambal oelek
- 1/4 tsp of garlic powder
- 1/4 tsp of ginger powder
- Kosher salt

Instructions

1. Stir together the sambal oelek, shallots, garlic, ginger, cilantro stems, coriander, turmeric, curry powder, and 3 tbsp of water in a blender or food processor until smooth. If the ingredients aren't coming together into a smooth paste, add another 1–2 tsp of water.
2. A big saucepan should be used to heat oil over medium heat. Put in the paste and simmer for around four to five minutes

while stirring regularly. Mix in the coconut milk and broth with a whisk, and then sprinkle on some Kosher salt. Put in a pot and fill with water, then bring to a boil. Cook on low for 20–25 minutes. If you want to add fish sauce and brown sugar, simmer for another 5 minutes.

3. In the meantime, bring a medium pot of water to a boil and cook the eggs. The heat should be reduced to a "hard simmer," or a very low boil. Gently place eggs in water and simmer for exactly 7 minutes. Get the eggs out of the water and into an ice bath using a slotted spoon (bowl filled with very icy water). After the eggs have cooled completely, peel them and cut them in half gently.

4. Meanwhile, in a large pan over medium heat, heat the oil and fry the spicy pork. Break up the pork into small pieces as it cooks and season with Kosher salt; cook until no pink remains, about 6-7 minutes. Cook for a further minute after adding the sambal oelek, garlic powder, and ginger powder. Take off the heat and lay aside until the soup is finished cooking.

5. Noodles should be boiled in boiling water for 2–3 minutes, or until they are al dente, during the last minutes the ramen soup simmers (if you cook too long, they will turn to mush).

6. Share the broth among the bowls. Put in some ramen noodles, some spicy pork, some onions, and some cilantro for flavor and presentation. Add lime wedges before serving. Enjoy right now.

RAMEN WITH CHARRED PORK

Prep time: 40 minutes

Total time: 60 minutes

Serving: 4

Ingredients

- 6 cups of low-sodium chicken broth
- 6 thick slices fresh ginger
- 4 cloves garlic
- 2 scallions, cut into thirds, + sliced scallions for topping
- 3/4 cup of dried shiitake mushrooms
- 1 tbsp of low-sodium soy sauce
- 1 tbsp of Shaoxing rice wine or dry sherry
- Kosher salt and freshly ground pepper
- 3 tbsp of hoisin sauce
- 1 tsp of toasted sesame oil
- 4 boneless pork chops
- 2 large eggs
- 1 1/2 lb. of fresh ramen noodles
- 1 5-oz. of package baby spinach
- Shichimi togarashi , for topping

Directions

1. Put the shiitake mushrooms, soy sauce, rice wine, and 2 and a half cups of of water in a large saucepan. Add the sliced ginger, 3 crushed garlic cloves, 2 scallions, and the chicken broth. Keep covered and heat until boiling. Cover and boil over low heat for 35 to 40 minutes, or until mushrooms are tender and broth is delicious. Add salt and pepper as need.
2. In the meantime, in a medium bowl, mix together the hoisin sauce, sesame oil, minced ginger, minced garlic, a bit of salt, and a few grinds of pepper. After forking the pork chops all

over, put them to the bowl and turn to coat. Infuse for 15 to 20 minutes at room temperature.

3. Prepare an indoor grill or outside fire for medium heat. The pork chops should take around 2 minutes every side on the grill. Take off the heat and set the meat on a chopping board for 5 minutes. Prepare the pork chops by slicing them thinly.

4. In a separate, big saucepan, bring water to a boil. Return to a simmer, add the eggs in their shells, and cook for 6 1/2 minutes. Fill a sink with cold water and let it drain. To prepare, first peel and halve the eggs.

5. Bring the water back up to a rolling boil. Throw in the noodles and boil them according to the package directions, making sure to mix them frequently. After draining, divide the contents amongst four dishes.

6. The broth should be strained into a new saucepan using a fine-mesh strainer. Throw in the spinach and wilt it down a bit with some stirring. Place the noodles in a bowl and pour the broth and spinach over them. Top with the pork, cut scallions, and eggs.

PERFECT INSTANT RAMEN

Prep time: 4 minutes

Total time: 10 minutes

Serving: 1

Ingredients

- 1 pack ramen noodles with flavor packet
- 1 large egg
- ½ tsp of butter
- 2slices American cheese
- ¼ tsp of toasted sesame seeds

- ½ scallion, green part only, thinly sliced

Preparation

1. In a little saucepan, bring 2.5 cups of of water to a boil. Stir in the noodles and simmer for 2 minutes. After 30 further seconds of cooking, add the flavor package and mix.
2. Take the pan off the burner and gently drop in the egg. Instead of stirring, pull the noodles over the egg and let it sit for a minute to poach.
3. Add the butter, cheese, and sesame seeds, then carefully move everything to a serving dish. Add the scallions as a garnish if you like.

PORK & RAMEN STIR-FRY

Prep time: 14 minutes

Total time:30 minutes

Serving: 4

Ingredients

- 1/4 cup of reduced-sodium soy sauce
- 2 tbsp of ketchup
- 2 tbsp of Worcestershire sauce
- 2 tsp of sugar
- 1/4 tsp of crushed red pepper flakes
- 3 tsp of canola oil, divided
- 1-lb. of boneless pork loin chops, cut
- 1 cup of fresh broccoli florets
- 4 cups of coleslaw mix
- 1 bamboo shoots, drained
- 4 garlic cloves, minced
- 2 packages ramen noodles

Directions

1. Mix the first five ingredients in a small bowl and stir to mix. Two tbsp of of oil should be heated over medium heat in a big pan. Mix in the pork and stir-fry for two to three minutes, or until the meat is no longer pink. Toss out of the pan.
2. Keep the skillet clean and use the leftover oil to stir-fry 3 minutes' worth of broccoli. Broccoli should be cooked until it is crisp-tender, so add coleslaw mix, bamboo shoots, and garlic and continue to stir-fry for another 3 to 4 minutes. In a saucepan, mix the soy sauce, water, and pork and bring to a simmer.
3. In the meantime, prepare the noodles as directed on the package, tossing or storing the flavor packets for later. Noodles should be drained before being added to the meat mixture.

BREAKFAST RAMEN NOODLES

Prep time: 5 minutes

Total time: 20 minutes

Serving: 2

Ingredients

- 3-oz. of ramen noodle soup
- 1 tbsp of butter, divided
- ½ cup of chopped bell peppers
- ½ cup of chopped onions
- 4 slices Black Forest deli ham
- 4 large eggs, beaten
- salt and pepper, as need

Instructions

1. Cook the ramen noodles in boiling water according to the package directions, omitting the spice packet, in a small to medium-sized saucepan.
2. The noodles should be drained and returned to the saucepan. Toss in a half spoonful of butter and the spice packet's contents and mix until the butter is melted and the seasoning is dispersed throughout the noodles.
3. The last half tbsp of of butter should be melted over medium heat in a large nonstick pan (I use a 12-inch skillet). Put in the onions and peppers. For about 4 minutes, while stirring occasionally, sauté until tender.
4. For about 2 to 3 minutes, while stirring regularly, the ham should be heated thoroughly and gently browned.
5. Stir in the noodles and the eggs. Wait until the eggs are set, stirring occasionally. Salt and pepper as need, if necessary.

SUKIYAKI BEEF RAMEN

Prep time: 20 minutes

Total time: 35 minutes

Serving: 4

Ingredients

- 4 cups of water
- 1 cup of mirin sweet rice wine
- 1 cup of sake
- ¾ cup of soy sauce
- ½ cup of sugar
- 2 lb. of thinly sliced lean beef such as sirloin
- ½ cup of Shoyu Tare
- 5 cups of any type clear soup
- 1⅓ lb. of fresh noodles ⅓ lb. of per bowl

- negi

Instructions

1. The water, mirin, sake, soy sauce, and sugar for the sukiyaki topping should be mixd in a large pot. Bring the liquid to a simmer over medium heat. After the oil has heated, add the steak and fry for three minutes. Take the sukiyaki meat off the stove and leave it in the sauce.
2. Now that you have everything prepped, bring a big pot of water to a boil over medium heat.
3. Start by filling your ramen bowls with boiling water to a minimum of halfway. The bowls shouldn't be scorching, but they should be hot to the touch. Get rid of the hot water and dry the bowls with some paper towels or a clean cloth.
4. Add the tare to a medium pot along with the soup. Mix, then heat to a moderate simmer.
5. Put the noodles into the big saucepan of boiling water. It just takes approximately two minutes to prepare ramen if it has been chopped to the customary thickness of around 1 mm.
6. Ladle the broth into the ramen bowls about 30 seconds before the noodles are done cooking.
7. You should rinse the noodles under cold running water and then drain and shake out as much excess water as possible. Put a few noodles in every serving of soup, taking care to avoid messes.
8. Spread the sukiyaki meat evenly over the ramen, then sprinkle with negi. It's fine to add some of the sukiyaki sauce, but keep in mind that it has a very robust flavor. Don't wait around; serve right away.

SPICY MISO RAMEN

Prep time: 10 minutes

Total time: 40 minutes

Serving: 3

Ingredients

- 8 oz. of ground chicken or pork
- 2 Tbsp of. neutral cooking oil
- 6 to 8 oz. of thinly sliced shiitake mushrooms, stems removed
- ½ cup of minced shallots
- 4 garlic cloves, minced
- 1 Tbsp of. freshly grated ginger
- 3 Tbsp of. white miso paste
- 2 Tbsp of. lower-sodium soy sauce
- 2 Tbsp of. rice vinegar
- 1 Tbsp of. hot chili oil
- 6 cups of low sodium chicken or vegetable broth
- 2 packs dry ramen noodles
- 1 cup of sweet corn
- 3 soft-boiled eggs, halved
- Thinly sliced green onions for garnish
- Toasted sesame seeds for garnish

Instructions

1. Pre-heat a large pot, such as a Dutch oven, over medium heat. Grease gently and add chicken or pork once the pan is hot (or vegetarian alternative). After 4 or 5 minutes, use a wooden spoon to break up the meat into smaller pieces and stir it. Place the meat in a dish and put it in the fridge.
2. Put the mushrooms and oil in the pan. Bake for 5 minutes, or until the vegetables are golden and soft. Cook the aromatics

(the shallots, garlic, and ginger) for two to three minutes after stirring them in.

3. Add the miso paste, soy sauce, rice vinegar, and chile oil, and mix well. Bring the mixture to a boil after adding the broth. Turn down the heat to medium-low and simmer very slowly for 20 minutes.
4. Reheat the stock and toss in the noodles. Noodles should be cooked for 3 minutes, or according to package directions, to get an al dente texture. Incorporate the cooked meat and corn into the mash.
5. Serve ramen in bowls and top with a soft-boiled egg, some green onions, and some toasted sesame seeds. Add additional chile oil if you want things spicy.

RAMEN NOODLE BRATWURST SOUP

Prep time: 5 minutes

Total time: 20 minutes

Serving: 4

Ingredients

- 2 tbsp of grapeseed oil
- 1 lb. of bratwurst, diced small
- 4 packages chicken flavor ramen soup
- 2 tbsp of chopped fresh parsley or chives

Directions

1. In a pan, heat the grapeseed oil over medium heat. Bratwursts are best after a brief fry and a quick drain on paper towels.
2. So, start by bringing 8 cups of water to a boil. The ramen noodles should be added and stirred in, then left to simmer

for 2 minutes. Add the chicken seasoning packet and continue cooking for another 2 minutes, stirring occasionally. Put in the bratwurst and let it rest for a covered minute.

3. Garnish with fresh parsley or chives and serve immediately.

PULLED PORK RAMEN

Prep time:20 minutes

Total time: 2 hours 20 minutes

Serving: 4

Ingredients

Pork and broth

- 1 pork shoulder roast
- 1 litre chicken stock
- ¼ cup of soy sauce
- 3 tbsp of rice vinegar
- 2 tbsp of sesame oil
- ¼ cup of brown sugar
- 1 tbsp of fresh ginger

Additions

- 100g ramen noodles
- 4 jammy soft-boiled eggs
- 1 bunch enoki mushrooms
- 4-6 shiitake mushrooms
- 1-2 spring onions, green part only, finely sliced

Directions

1. Throw the meat into a slow cooker or a baking dish with high sides. Add the other ingredients for the broth, except the

sesame oil, and pour over the top. Fork-tender pork may be achieved by covering the dish and cooking it for 4 to 6 hours on the low setting of a slow cooker or in an oven preheated to 160 degrees Celsius.

2. Take the pork out of the soup and shred it into a separate bowl.

3. After the stock has been warming for a few minutes, add the mushrooms and let them simmer for 1-2 minutes. Put a frying pan over medium heat while the mushrooms cook in the residual heat of the liquid. A gentle caramelization on the edges of the pulled pork should take around 1 to 3 minutes in the pan after you add the sesame oil. For added crunch, you can use 1 tbsp of brown sugar to sprinkle over the top before baking.

4. Ladle the broth into individual bowls. When the broth is ready, toss in the noodles and let them to warm through before adding the pulled pork, soft-boiled egg halves (two halves per serving), and spring onion. Ensure that the food is served hot.

SPICY PORK RAMEN NOODLE SOUP

Prep time:20 minutes

Total time: 5 hours

Serving: 4

Ingredients

- 2 tbsp of olive oil
- 2.2 lbs rolled pork shoulder
- ¼ tsp of salt
- ¼ tsp of pepper
- 8 ½ cups of chicken

- 1 onion cut
- 2 carrots peeled
- 1 stick of celery
- 3 cloves garlic
- 1 thumb-sized piece of ginger
- 2 tbsp of mirin
- 3 tbsp of soy sauce
- 2 tbsp of Gochujang Paste
- 1 red chilli roughly sliced
- 4 large eggs
- 7 oz dried ramen noodles
- 1 leek - sliced
- 3 packed cups of baby spinach leaves
- 1 tsp of sesame seeds
- 1 tsp of black sesame seeds
- Small bunch spring onions
- 1 tsp of red chilli flakes

Instructions

1. Set the oven temperature to 300F/150C. Heat 1 tbsp of of oil in a large casserole dish over high heat.
2. Put the pork in the pan with the heated oil and season it with salt and pepper. Close off all openings.
3. Add the stock to the meat and stir.
4. Put in the entire carrot, celery, garlic, and ginger, along with the onion.
5. Now stir in the mirin, soy sauce, gochujang, and red pepper flakes. Raise the temperature to high, then cover and bake for 4 hours.
6. Put the pork on a cutting board and remove the pan from the oven. Take the fat off the top and throw it away. Two forks can be used to shred the meat.
7. Strain the cooking liquid using a strainer set over a big basin. Remove the liquid from the pan and add it back to the meat

while discarding the veggies. Turn the heat on low and leave it on.

8. The eggs should be cooked in a small pan. It's as simple as covering with cold water. Simmer for 6 minutes after bringing to a boil.

9. To end the cooking process, take the eggs off the fire and put them in a dish of cold water.

10. In order to cook dry noodles, you need put them in a pot of boiling water for around 5 minutes. Afterwards, decant, rinse in cold water (to prevent sticking), and set aside.

11. In a frying pan, heat the remaining oil.

12. Fry the leek for 5 minutes while turning a few times and seasoning with salt and pepper.

13. Place the spinach in the pan and move the leeks to one side of the pan. Give it a minute to wilt.

14. Place the noodles in four separate dishes. Hot broth, pork shreds, leeks, spinach, and carrot sticks on top.

15. To prepare, peel the two eggs and cut them in half lengthwise. Separate them in half and put one half in every bowl.

16. Sprinkle the white and black sesame seeds and the chili flakes over the soup, and then top with the spring onions.

EASY SHRIMP RAMEN SOUP

Prep time:10 minutes

Total time: 20 minutes

Serving: 4

Ingredients

- 1-2 tbsp of olive oil
- 8 oz. of sliced mushrooms
- 1 large carrot, grated

- 4 cloves garlic, minced
- 4 cups of low sodium broth/stock of choice
- 1 tbsp of freshly grated ginger
- 1 tsp of low sodium soy sauce
- 1 tsp of sesame oil
- 2 packages ramen noodles
- 1 lb. of large raw shrimp
- Chopped green onions and cilantro for garnish, optional

Instructions

1. Brown the mushrooms and carrots in olive oil in a large saucepan over medium heat for about 5 minutes, or until the mushrooms are soft and the carrots are translucent. For a further 30 seconds while stirring, add the garlic. Stir in the broth, ginger, soy sauce, and sesame oil. A boil should be reveryed while the pot is covered.
2. When the water is boiling, throw in the shrimp and noodles. Put the lid on and let it boil for three minutes. Garnish with chopped green onions and cilantro, if using.

SPICY SHRIMP RAMEN BOWLS

Prep time:10 minutes

Total time: 20 minutes

Serving: 4

Ingredients

- 3 pkgs ramen, seasoning packet discarded
- 1 1/2 lbs large shrimp peeled and deveined
- 6 cups of chicken, vegetable or seafood stock
- 2 tbsp of olive oil
- 1-2 tbsp of sriracha

- 3 tbsp of soy sauce
- 3 cloves garlic minced
- 1 tsp of grated fresh ginger
- 1 1/2 tbsp of brown sugar
- 2 cups of shredded green cabbage
- 3/4 cup of carrots thinly sliced
- 3/4 cup of sweet peppers thinly sliced
- 1/2 cup of onion thinly sliced
- juice of 1 lime
- Cilantro

Instructions

1. Put 1 tbsp of of olive oil into the pan and heat it over medium. Cook the shrimp for 1-2 minutes per side, or until they turn pink and firm. Dedicate a separate space for
2. Put 1 tbsp of of olive oil in a big saucepan and set it over medium heat. Cook the vegetables for two to three minutes before adding the garlic and ginger and cooking for an additional minute. Blend together the stock, soy sauce, brown sugar, lime juice, and sriracha. Simmer for 8 minutes at a low boil after being brought to a quick boil.
3. After the soup has simmered for a further 2–3 minutes, add the dried ramen noodles. Turn off the heat, divide into dishes, add the shrimp, and top with cilantro.

SEAFOOD SHIO RAMEN

Prep time:10 minutes

Total time: 20 minutes

Serving: 4

Ingredients

- Vegetable oil for frying
- 12 to 16 large scallops
- ½ cup of Shio Tare
- 5 cups of any type clear soup
- 1⅓ lb. of noodles fresh
- 4 tbsp of shrimp oil
- 4 Salted Eggs halved
- Negi

Instructions

1. In a large skillet, heat some vegetable oil over medium heat. The scallops should be lightly sautéed on both sides until barely done. Put aside for a moment.
2. Now that you have everything prepped, bring a big pot of water to a boil over medium heat.
3. Start by filling your ramen bowls with boiling water to a minimum of halfway. The bowls shouldn't be scorching, but they should be hot to the touch. Get rid of the hot water and dry the bowls with some paper towels or a clean cloth.
4. Add the tare to a medium pot along with the soup. Mix, then heat to a moderate simmer.
5. Put the noodles into the big saucepan of boiling water. It just takes approximately two minutes to prepare ramen if it has been chopped to the customary thickness of around 1 mm.
6. Every bowl of ramen should have 1 tbsp of of shrimp oil.
7. Ladle the broth into the ramen bowls about 30 seconds before the noodles are done cooking.
8. You should rinse the noodles under cold running water and then drain and shake out as much excess water as possible. Put a few noodles in every serving of soup, taking care to avoid messes.
9. Arrange 3–4 scallops, a salted egg, and a sprinkling of negi in a tidy pile on the ramen. Don't wait around; serve right away.

CREAMY SALMON PASTA

Prep time:10 minutes

Total time: 20 minutes

Serving: 4

Ingredients

- 0.75 lb. of fettuccine pasta
- 1 lb. of fresh salmon fillet
- 1 ½ cups of cherry tomatoes
- 1 cup of baby spinach leaves, packed
- Kosher salt
- Ground black pepper
- Olive oil
- Freshly grated parmesan cheese

Creamy Sauce

- 4 tbsp of unsalted butter
- 3 cloves fresh garlic, minced
- 1 cup of heavy cream - + more as need
- 2 cups of freshly grated parmesan cheese
- Ground black pepper as need

Instructions

1. Get the oven up to temperature, preferably 400 degrees F. Prepare an aluminum foil-lined baking sheet. Put aside for a moment.
2. Pasta should be prepared in heavily salted water, according package instructions. Get rid of the water and put it away.
3. Salmon with roasted tomatoes: The skin can stay on the salmon fillet when you lay it on the baking sheet. Apply a mixture of 1 tbsp of olive oil, 1/2 tsp of salt, and 1/4 tsp of freshly ground black pepper to the salmon and rub it all over.

Arrange the cherry tomatoes in a single layer on the baking sheet, then drizzle with olive oil and season with salt. Cook at 400 degrees F for 10 to 12 minutes, or until the salmon is opaque and the tomatoes are blistered. To take out of the oven. Fork-flake the salmon (discard the skin). Put aside for a moment.

4. To whip up the velvety sauce, do the following: Over medium heat, add the minced garlic to the melted butter in a large pan. In a pan over medium heat, cook the spices for 1-2 minutes. After that, pour in the heavy cream and reduce the heat to a low simmer. Sprinkle some freshly ground black pepper and freshly grated Parmesan cheese on top. Bring to a simmer and whisk often until melted and mixd. Cream can be thinned out if it becomes too thick.

5. Mix the fettuccine with the sauce once it has been cooked. You may now add the spinach and toss it a couple more times to wilt it. Flake in the cooked fish and toss with the tomatoes.

6. Sprinkle with some freshly grated parmesan. Don't wait around; serve right away. Enjoy!

CREAMY VEGETARIAN MISO RAMEN WITH SOYA & DASHI BROTH

Prep time:10 minutes

Total time: 20 minutes

Serving: 2

Ingredients

Ramen

- 160g dried ramen noodles or egg noodles
- 500ml of vegetable stock

- 5cm x 5cm of dried kombu
- 250ml unsweetened soy milk
- 1 tbsp of of sake
- 2 tsp of of mirin
- 1 tsp of of Japanese soy sauce
- 1 tbsp of or white or brown miso, or homemade miso

Toppings

- 90g pack of baby pak choi
- 100g of beansprouts
- 3 spring onions, finely chopped
- 2 tbsp of of frozen sweetcorn, defrosted
- 1 boiled egg, shelled and halved
- 1 tbsp of of fried onions
- Japanese chill oil

Instructions

1. At first, you must prepare the soup. Put the kombu in the vegetable stock and let it soak for at least 30 minutes.
2. In a saucepan, bring the stock together with the kombu to a boil. Once the stock has begun to boil, remove the kombu and add the soy milk, sake (if using), mirin, and soy sauce.
3. Take it off the heat and add the miso all at once, stirring it in. More than 1 tbsp of can be added if desired; simply season as need as you go. Whether white or red miso is utilized determines the intensity of flavor.
4. Baby pak choi should be steamed for 3–5 minutes and beansprouts should be blanched in boiling water for 1–2 minutes. Toss together any other condiments you'll be using.
5. After the noodles have been cooked, divide them evenly between two serving dishes. Use the soup to cover the noodles. Put in the bean sprouts and pak choi.

6. Last but not least, finish with salad onions, sweetcorn, an egg, some crispy onions, and either the chilli oil or shichimi togarashi (if using).

GYOZA CHILLI NOODLE SOUP

Prep time:5 minutes

Total time: 15 minutes

Serving: 2

Ingredients

- 3 spring onions finely chopped
- 2 tbsp of sesame oil
- 2 tbsp of tamari or soy sauce
- 800 ml vegetable stock made with boiling water and stock cube
- 3 cloves garlic minced
- 1 thumb sized piece fresh ginger grated
- 1 large red chilli
- 1 tbsp of brown sugar
- 100 g noodles rice, ribbon
- 5 tenderstem
- 6 gyozas I used yukata vegan gyozas
- 1 tsp of sesame seeds to top, optional

Instructions

1. Mix the brown sugar, sesame oil, tamari, and chopped ginger in a small bowl.
2. Cook the spring onions in the dressing for about 3 minutes in a hot skillet before adding the vegetable stock.
3. The gyozas should be fried in a little sesame oil over high heat for three to four minutes until they are golden and crisp,

and then steamed for the same amount of time with the lid on.

4. The rice noodles and tender stem should be added to the stock in the last 5 minutes of cooking, and the pan should be covered so that the contents gently steam for about 4 minutes.
5. To serve, place some soup and noodles in a dish, then add some gyozas and the delicate stem and sprinkle with some more spring onions, chili flakes, and tamari, if desired.

CAMPBELL'S TUNA NOODLE CASSEROLE

Prep time:10 minutes

Total time: 45 minutes

Serving: 8

Ingredients

- 4 cups of hot cooked medium egg noodles
- 2 Condensed Cream of Mushroom Soup
- 2 tuna, drained
- 2 cups of frozen peas
- 1 cup of milk
- 2 tbsp of dry bread crumbs
- 1 tbsp of butter, melted

Directions

1. Get the oven up to temperature, preferably 400 degrees F. (200 degrees C).
2. Prepare a 3-quart casserole dish by mixing together cooked noodles, condensed soup, tuna, peas, and milk.
3. Put in an oven that has been prepared to 350 degrees for 30 minutes; stir occasionally until hot.

4. To make the topping, mix the bread crumbs with the melted butter in a dish and sprinkle it over the tuna casserole before returning it to the oven for another 5 minutes, or until the bread crumbs are golden and crispy.

SHOYU RAMEN

Prep time:20 minutes

Total time: 20 minutes

Serving: 2

Ingredients

- 1 piece kombu seaweed
- ½ cup of bonito flakes
- 1 pouch Nona Lim chicken stock
- 1 tbsp of sesame oil
- 1 clove garlic, finely grated
- 2 tsp of grated ginger
- 3 tbsp of soy sauce
- 1 tsp of mirin
- 1 pack Nona Lim Noodles
- 2 pieces of menma
- 4 slices chashu
- 6 slices of narutomaki
- 2 pieces of nori
- 1 soft boiled egg, halved
- 2 scallions, thinly sliced
- 1 tbsp of sesame seeds

Directions

1. Get the dashi going. Simmer kombu in 2 cups of of water in a small saucepan over medium heat.

2. Start by heating 2 cups of of water with the kombu in a small saucepan over medium heat. Do not boil, but simmer.
3. Once the kombu has been boiled for a few minutes, remove it and replace it with the bonito flakes. Ten minutes after it starts simmering, set it aside.
4. Put the liquid through a mesh strainer. You have obtained dashi at this time.
5. Chicken stock and dashi stock should be mixd in a separate skillet and kept warm over low heat.
6. First, prepare the tare by heating the sesame oil and then sautéing the garlic and ginger until fragrant. Turn off the heat and stir in the mirin and soy sauce.
7. One spoon at a time, add the tare to the dashi stock until seasoned as need.
8. Prepare the ramen noodles as directed on the box.
9. While waiting, prepare a soft-boiled egg by boiling one and peeling it after it cools.
10. Partially fill two bowls with the rice and then pour the broth over the top.
11. Sprinkle menma, chashu, and narutomaki on top of every dish. The egg can be served on top after being sliced. Green onions, sesame oil, and chili oil (if you like things spicy) make for a great garnish.

TSUKEMEN

Prep time:20 minutes

Total time: 7 hours

Serving: 2

Ingredients

Broth

- 2 lb pork bones
- 1 lb chicken feet
- 2 inch ginger knob smashed
- 6 scallions white ends only
- 6 cloves garlic smashed

Shoyu tare

- ½ cup of soy sauce
- 1 tsp of mirin
- 1 tsp of sake
- 1 garlic minced
- 2 tsp of ginger minced
- 1 scallion white end only
- 2x2 inch kombu
- 1 oz. of bonito flakes

Tsukemen

- 4 oz. of pork belly cut into bite-size chunks
- 1 tsp of garlic minced
- 1 tsp of ginger minced
- ¼ cup of all-purpose flour
- 3 cups of pork broth
- 3 tbsp of tare
- ½ cup of bonito flakes
- 1 tbsp of dried sardine powder
- ½ tsp of salt

Remaining ingredients

- 2 packets thick ramen noodles
- 6 oz. of chashu
- 2 soft boiled eggs
- ½ cup of thinly shaved red onion
- 2 lime wedges

- 2 tbsp of chopped scallions

Instructions

1. Get the stock going. Make sure your pork bones and chicken feet are clean before throwing them in the instant pot. The bones should be submerged in water and pressure cooked for at least 10 minutes on high. Allow the pressure to drop and strain the bones. It's time to clean the instant pot and give the bones a quick rinse in cold water. Add the ginger, scallion ends, and garlic to the saucepan with the bones. Add enough water to the saucepan so that it comes up two inches above the ingredients. Do a one-hour high-pressure cook in the instant pot.

2. Turn the instant pot off and remove the lid. Shake the pot and shatter any bones that are fragile enough to do so. Keep cooking for another hour on high heat. Turn off the pressure and give the bones another stir to see if you can break any more of them down. Proceed in this manner for a total of 6 hours. Remove the meat and vegetables from the stock and set them aside.

3. To tare, just. Bring the tare ingredients to a boil in a small saucepot over medium heat. For the next 5 minutes, keep the heat on low and simmer the mixture. Use a strainer to remove the unwanted substances. Wait for it to cool down.

4. Heat a medium saucepot over medium-high heat. During the last 3 minutes, add the pork belly pieces and simmer until browned. Stir in the garlic, ginger, and flour to coat. To prevent the pork belly from drying out, use 2 tbsp of of oil even if you're using lean pork belly.

5. Throw in the saved meat pieces, 3 tbsp of of tare, 1/2 cup of bonito flakes, and 1 tbsp of of dried sardine powder, along with 3 cups of of stock. Bring to a boil and cook for 10

minutes or until thickened, stirring periodically. Add a pinch of salt as need to the tsukemen.

6. Follow the package instructions for cooking ramen noodles. Sift and flush with cold water. Divide the noodles between two bowls and top every with half an egg, some sliced chashu, some shaved red onion, some soft cooked noodles, and a wedge of lime. Place a serving of tsukemen in every of two dishes and sprinkle every with a handful of sliced scallions.

BEST TUNA CASSEROLE

Prep time:10 minutes

Total time: 30 minutes

Serving: 6

Ingredients

- 12 oz. of egg noodles
- 10.5 oz. of condensed cream of mushroom soup
- 2 cups of shredded Cheddar cheese, divided
- 5 oz. of tuna, drained
- 1 cup of frozen green peas
- 4.5 oz. of sliced mushrooms
- ¼ cup of chopped onion
- 1 cup of crushed potato chips

Directions

1. Put some salt in a big saucepan of water and bring it to a rolling boil. Noodles made from eggs should be boiled for 7 to 9 minutes, or until they are soft but still have some bite to them.

2. In the meantime, set the oven temperature to 425 degrees F. (220 degrees C).
3. In a large bowl, mix the cooked noodles, can of condensed soup, 1 cup of the shredded cheese, the canned tuna, the frozen peas, the canned mushrooms, and the chopped onion. Place in a 9x13-inch baking dish and sprinkle with the potato chip crumbs and the remaining 1 cup of cheese.
4. For around 15 to 20 minutes in a preheated oven, or until the cheese is melted and bubbling.

FURIKAKE SALMON AND KUNG PAO BRUSSELS SPROUTS RAMEN

Prep time:10 minutes

Total time: 30 minutes

Serving: 3

Ingredients

Salmon:

- 2 salmon fillets
- 2 T mayo
- 2 T soy sauce
- 1 - 2 T furikake seasoning

Brussel sprouts:

- 2 lbs Brussels sprouts, trimmed and halved
- 1 T Olive Oil
- 2 T soy sauce
- 1 T maple syrup
- 1 T rice vinegar

- 2 T sesame oil
- 1 - 2 T sriracha

Ramen:

- Lotus Foods Ramen with Miso Soup

Directions

1. Turn oven temperature up to 400 degrees F.
2. Season Brussels sprouts with salt and pepper and toss them with 1 T olive oil. Toss in the oven and roast for 20 minutes, or until the meat is almost done. While the Brussels sprouts are in the oven, you may create the sauce. Return the tossed Brussels to the oven for another 8-10 minutes, tossing once, to let the sauce to caramelize and soak.
3. The fillets should be placed skin-side down on a parchment-lined pan. In a small bowl, stir together the mayonnaise and soy sauce. The meat side was liberally spread. Furikake should be sprinkled evenly over the mayonnaise-coated fish. Bake with Brussels sprouts for 12-15 minutes, or until fish is flaky.
4. The ramen should be prepared and the broth should be divided among bowls. Prepare a bed of Brussels sprouts and then top with salmon. Use pickled ginger as a garnish.

RAMEN COLESLAW

Prep time:15minutes

Total time: 30 minutes

Serving: 4

Ingredients

- ½ medium head cabbage, shredded

- 5 green onions, chopped
- 3 oz. of chicken flavored ramen noodles
- ¼ cup of sliced almonds
- 2 tbsp of sesame seeds

Dressing:

- 3 tbsp of white wine vinegar
- 2 tbsp of vegetable oil
- 2 tbsp of white sugar
- ½ tsp of salt
- ½ tsp of ground black pepper

Directions

1. Make sure your oven is at least halfway up to temperature (at least 350 degrees F).
2. Put the ramen noodles, green onions, and cabbage in a large salad dish.
3. On a baking sheet, scatter the almonds and sesame seeds.
4. Put into an oven that has been prepared to 400 degrees and bake for about 10 minutes, or until a light brown color has developed.
5. While that's going on, prepare the dressing: In a medium bowl, mix the vinegar, oil, sugar, salt, pepper, and spice package.
6. Toss the cabbage mixture with the dressing to coat evenly. Toast some almonds and sesame seeds and sprinkle them on top.

SOFT SHELL CRAB

Prep time:15 minutes

Total time: 30 minutes

Serving: 1

Ingredients

- Soft shell crab
- Ingredients from your favorite recipes

Instructions

1. The flavor of a meal can change dramatically based on factors including the components employed, the technique employed, and the type of dish being prepared.
2. Choose a recipe that will bring out the best in the food's natural flavors, and have fun trying out new ones!

THAI CURRY BEEF 'RAMEN'

Prep time:15minutes

Total time: 35 minutes

Serving: 4

Ingredients

- 2 tsp of sesame or vegetable oil
- 1 lb extra lean ground beef
- 3 tbsp of Thai red curry paste
- 2 red Thai chili peppers, seeded
- 1 tbsp of low-sodium soy sauce
- 2 tsp of EVERY liquid honey, and minced ginger
- 1 tsp of minced garlic

- 4 cups of sodium-reduced chicken broth
- 1 coconut milk
- 1 tbsp of fresh lime juice
- 1/2 tsp of salt
- 150 g whole-grain spaghettini
- 4 baby bok choy, halved
- 1 red bell pepper, thinly sliced
- 8 oz (250 g) button mushrooms, thinly sliced
- 4 cups of lightly packed baby spinach
- 1 cup of fresh basil leaves, torn
- 1/4 cup of chopped roasted peanuts
- Lime wedges

Instructions

1. Oil should be heated in a big pot or Dutch oven over medium heat. Add the ground beef and simmer for 5 minutes, breaking it up with a spoon as it cooks, until browned. Using a slotted spoon, remove the meat to a platter, cover, and set aside.

2. Whisk together the curry paste, chili peppers, soy sauce, honey, ginger, and garlic in a saucepan. To intensify the crimson color, cook the mixture for an additional minute or two. Add the salt and then the coconut milk, lime juice, and broth. Put on high heat and whisk in the spaghetti until it is completely submerged. Keep the lid on and the heat at medium. For 5 minutes in a pot over medium heat, stirring regularly, you may get food that is soft but still has some bite to it.

3. Put the meat back in the pan and mix it all together. The bok choy, pepper, mushrooms, and spinach should be layered over the soup. In a covered pot, simmer for 5 minutes, or until tender. Mix by tossing.

4. Separate the noodles and veggies into four large dishes. Pour some of the broth over the top. Add chopped basil and peanuts as a garnish. Add lime wedges before serving.

BEST STEAK MARINADE IN EXISTENCE

Prep time:15minutes

Total time: 15 minutes

Serving: 8

Ingredients

- ½ cup of olive oil
- ⅓ cup of soy sauce
- ⅓ cup of fresh lemon juice
- ¼ cup of Worcestershire sauce
- 3 tbsp of dried basil
- 1 ½ tbsp of garlic powder
- 1 ½ tbsp of dried parsley flakes
- 1 tsp of ground white pepper
- 1 tsp of dried minced garlic
- ¼ tsp of hot pepper sauce

Directions

Blend for 30 seconds at high speed to incorporate the white pepper, minced garlic, olive oil, basil, garlic powder, soy sauce, lemon juice, Worcestershire sauce parsley, and hot pepper sauce.

NOODLES ROMANOFF

Prep time: 5 minutes

Total time: 20 minutes

Serving: 1

Ingredients

- 1 cup of uncooked egg noodles
- 1/4 cup of sour cream
- 1 tbsp of butter, softened
- 1 tbsp of shredded Parmesan cheese
- 1/4 tsp of salt-free herb seasoning blend
- 1/8 tsp of garlic powder
- Dash pepper
- 1 tsp of minced chives

Directions

1. Prepare noodles as directed on the box. Meanwhile, whisk the sour cream, butter, Parmesan cheese, spice mix, garlic powder, and pepper together in a small basin.
2. Soak in cold water until ready to use. Add the sour cream mixture and stir to coat; reheat. Incorporate chopped chives.

STEAK AND ASPARAGUS TERIYAKI RAMEN

Prep time:15minutes

Total time: 25 minutes

Serving: 4

Ingredients

- Two packages ramen noodles
- 1 lb. of boneless skirt steak
- 1/4 cup of beef broth
- 3 tbsp of soy sauce; divided
- 1/2 tbsp of honey
- 1/4 tsp of garlic powder
- 1/4 tsp of crushed red pepper flakes
- 3 tsp of cornstarch
- 2 tsp of brown sugar
- 1 1/2 tsp of toasted sesame oil
- 6 tbsp of olive oil
- 1 large bundle of asparagus, chopped
- 1 tbsp of finely chopped ginger
- 4 cloves garlic, minced
- 4 green onions, thinly sliced

Instructions

1. Put the noodles in a big, heat-safe bowl. Put in a bowl, cover with boiling water, and set a small plate on top. Let sit for three to five minutes, or until the plate is removed and the food is fully cooked. Be sure to drain everything thoroughly before setting it away.
2. First, quarter the beef lengthwise, then cut it against the grain into thin slices. Every piece should be about 3 inches long.

3. Beef broth, 2 tbsp of soy sauce, honey, garlic powder, crushed red pepper flakes, cornstarch, brown sugar, and sesame oil should be whisked together in a medium basin and set away.

4. Pre-heat a large, nonstick pan over high heat and add the remaining olive oil (1 tbsp of). When the oil is sizzling hot, add half of the meat and sauté for 2 minutes, tossing once or twice, until browned on the outside but still juicy in the inside. Using a slotted spoon, remove the meat and place it in a large serving dish. Add another tbsp of of oil to the pan and repeat with the remaining meat. Put the beef in a serving dish and leave the pan on the stove.

5. Get a skillet hot and pour in 1 1/2 tsp of of oil. Then add the asparagus and simmer for approximately a minute, stirring often, until it softens. Turn the heat down to medium and throw in the garlic and ginger. Continue cooking for another 30 seconds, stirring regularly, or until *just browned and aromatic. Put 2 tbsp of of water in the pan and simmer over low heat, stirring regularly, for approximately a minute, or until the liquid has almost completely evaporated.

6. The beef broth mixture should be added to the pan. Warm for approximately a minute while stirring periodically, until thickened.

7. Coat the meat and add it to the pan. Place the steak in the center of a large serving plate and set the noodles to the side.

8. Scrub the pan clean, then heat the soy sauce and oil mixture over medium heat.

9. Toss in the ramen noodles and heat through, stirring occasionally (approximately a minute).

10. Place on a serving plate and top with sliced green onions. Get it on the table right away!

CHEESY MEATLOAF

Prep time:15minutes

Total time: 1 hours 15 minutes

Serving: 8

Ingredients

- 1 lb. of ground beef
- 1 lb. of ground pork
- 1 (1 oz. of) envelope dry onion soup mix
- 2 eggs, beaten
- 1 ½ cups of dry bread crumbs
- ground black pepper as need
- ¾ cup of water
- 2 cups of shredded mozzarella cheese, divided

Directions

1. Turn on oven to 350 degrees F. (175 degrees C).
2. Meat, pork, soup mix, eggs, bread crumbs, pepper, and water should all be mixed together in a big basin. Mix in a half a cup of the cheese. Mix everything thoroughly, then spoon half into a 9-by-5-inch loaf pan and spread evenly. Cover the meat loaf in the remaining 1 1/2 cups of of cheese. Cover with the second half of the meat loaf mixture.
3. Put in a 60minute baking time in a preheated oven. For best results, wait at least 10–15 minutes for serving.

VEGETABLE BEEF NOODLE SOUP

Prep time:10minutes

Total time: 30 minutes

Serving: 6

Ingredients

- 1 lb lean ground beef
- 1 small onion finely diced
- 1 tsp of kosher salt
- ½ tsp of black pepper
- 1 Italian style stewed tomatoes
- 2 beef broth
- 1 petite diced tomatoe
- 1 mixed vegetable drained
- 1 tsp of dried basil
- 1 tsp of dried parsley
- 1½ cups of uncooked egg noodles

Instructions

1. In a very large soup pot, brown the ground beef with the onion, salt, and pepper over medium heat. Shred meat while it simmers. Drain the fat once the meat is no longer pink in the middle.
2. The canned stewed tomatoes should be blended before being added to the soup saucepan with the meat.
3. Put in the veggies, herbs, beef stock, and diced tomatoes. Obtain a rolling boil.
4. Add the uncooked egg noodles to the boiling water and cover the saucepan. Reduce heat and simmer for 12-15 minutes, stirring occasionally.

CHINESE BEEF AND BROCCOLI NOODLES

Prep time:10minutes

Total time: 20 minutes

Serving: 4

Ingredients

- 350 oz beef rump or fillet, thinly sliced
- 1 1/2 tbsp of peanut or vegetable oil
- 2 garlic cloves, finely chopped
- 1/2 onion, finely sliced
- 1 large head broccoli, broken into small florets
- 400 oz egg noodles

Sauce:

- 1/2 cup of / 125 ml water
- 1 tbsp of cornflour / cornstarch
- 2 tbsp of dark soy sauce
- 1 1/2 tbsp of light soy sauce
- 1 1/2 tbsp of Chinese cooking wine
- 1 tsp of white sugar
- 1/8 tsp of Chinese five spice powder
- 1/2 tsp of sesame oil
- 1/4 tsp of pepper

Optional garnishes:

- Sesame seeds
- Chopped shallots

Instructions

1. To make the sauce, mix the water and cornstarch in a bowl. Then, incorporate the rest of the ingredients.
2. Beef: Add 1 1/2 tbsp of of sauce to a bowl. Mix.

3. Prepare a big pot of boiling water for the broccoli and noodles. Include broccoli, and heat for a minute. After 15 seconds, divide the noodles with a wooden spoon and quickly drain (no more than 1 minute in water).
4. In a big pan, warm the oil over high heat to prepare a stir-fry.
5. Insert garlic, and mix it in hastily. Toss in the onion and sauté for a minute, or until it begins to take on a brown hue.
6. To the pan, put meat and cook it until it turns brown.
7. Include the sauce, the broccoli, and the noodles. Stir for 1 1/2-2 minutes, until the sauce has thickened and coated the noodles. Shallots and sesame seeds (if used) can be sprinkled on top before serving.

RAMEN CHEESEBURGER CASSEROLE

Prep time:10minutes

Total time: 40 minutes

Serving: 6

Ingredients

- 1 85%-lean ground beef
- ¾ c. white onion, chopped
- 2 beef-flavored Ramen noodles
- 1 Hy-Vee diced tomatoes
- 1 Hy-Vee tomato sauce
- ½ c. Hy-Vee ketchup
- 2 tsp of. Hy-Vee yellow mustard
- 2 c. Hy-Vee smooth and cheesy loaf, cubed
- Desired toppers, such as: lettuce, dill pickles, and chopped tomatoe

Instructions

1. The oven has to be preheated to 350 degrees. Get out a 9-inch square baking dish that is nonstick. Before draining, beef should be browned and cooked through (to an internal temperature of 165 degrees).
2. The beef ramen noodles should be cut in half lengthwise. Mixd tomato paste, tomato sauce, ketchup, mustard, and ramen spice packets in a medium bowl and stir to mix. Spread 1 cup of the tomato mixture on the bottom of a casserole dish, then top with the ramen squares. The leftover tomato sauce should be spread on top. Incorporate cooked ground beef and onions into the dish.
3. Bake, covered, at 350 degrees for 25 minutes, or until bubbling and hot. Hy-cheesy, Vee's smooth bread should be placed on the plate. Keep it covered and in the oven for 5 minutes, examining it regularly to make sure the cheese has melted. If desired, top with chopped tomato, dill pickles, and lettuce.

CLASSIC BEEF AND NOODLES

Prep time:10minutes

Total time: 30 minutes

Serving: 4

Ingredients

- 1 tbsp of olive oil
- 1 lb. of beef stew meat
- 22 oz. of cream of mushroom soup
- 2 tbsp of onion dip mix
- 1 cup of beef broth
- 8 oz. of egg noodles

Instructions

Instant Pot directions:

1. Put olive oil in the saucepan of the pressure cooker and turn on the sauté setting. Brown the first half of the meat, flipping it over once. Take out of the stove and place on a platter. Second beef half should be browned.
2. preparation of beef skewers in an Instant Pot
3. Re-introduce the initial serving of meat to the pressure cooker, along with any collected fluids. Blend in some beef broth, onion dip mix, and cream of mushroom soup. Mixing is facilitated by stirring. If your Instant Pot keeps flashing "burn" warnings, try increasing the beef broth to 1 1/2 to 2 cups of.
4. Make sure the cover is on tight and cook at high pressure for 15 minutes. When finished, let go in their own time.
5. Instant pot beef stew with mushroom gravy.
6. Pasta should be cooked in a big pot of salted boiling water until al dente, drained, and left aside while the meat is cooking.
7. Serve the beef and mushroom combination on top of egg noodles or with the noodles mixed into the meat sauce.

Stove top directions:

1. Use the same technique of browning the meat in a heavy bottom saucepan over medium-high heat. Once everything has been put to the saucepan (excluding the egg noodles, which will need to be cooked in a separate pot), cover and braise at a simmer for at least an hour.

Slow cooker directions:

2. Use the same technique of browning the meat in a heavy bottom saucepan over medium-high heat. Mix the other ingredients, including the garlic, and place in a slow cooker (not the egg noodles which will need to be cooked

separately). Crockpot instructions: cover and cook for 2 hours on high or 6-8 hours on low.

VEGETABLE BEEF SOUP

Prep time: 20minutes

Total time: 1 hours 30 minutes

Serving: 8

Ingredients

- 1 1/2 lbs beef stew meat
- 2 1/2 Tbsp of olive oil, divided
- Salt and freshly ground black pepper
- 1 3/4 cups of chopped yellow onion
- 1 1/4 cups of peeled and chopped carrots
- 1 cup of chopped celery
- 1 1/2 Tbsp of minced garlic
- 8 cups of low-sodium beef broth or chicken broth
- 2 diced tomatoes
- 1 1/2 tsp of dried basil
- 1 tsp of dried oregano
- 1/2 tsp of dried thyme
- 1 lb red or yellow potatoes, chopped
- 1 1/2 cups of chopped green beans
- 1 1/2 cups of frozen corn
- 1 cup of frozen peas
- 1/3 cup of chopped fresh parsley

Instructions

1. In a large saucepan, heat 1 tbsp of of olive oil over medium heat.

2. Using paper towels, pat the beef dry, then season it with salt and pepper. Brown half of the steak in the saucepan for 4 minutes, flipping once.
3. Bring to a platter. To cook the other half of the meat, add another half a tbsp of of oil to the pan.
4. When the saucepan is empty, add another tbsp of of oil and the vegetables (onions, carrots, and celery) for a three-minute sauté before adding the garlic for an additional minute.
5. Add broth, tomatoes, meat that has been browned, herbs (basil, oregano, thyme), salt, and pepper. For 30 minutes, bring to a boil, then lower heat to low, cover, and simmer, stirring once or twice.
6. After 20 minutes, add the potatoes and continue simmering with the lid on (you can also add green beans with potatoes if you like them very soft).
7. Add the green beans, and continue simmering for another 15 minutes, or until the meat and vegetables are soft.
8. Add the corn and peas and cook for 5 minutes, or until hot. Warm the dish and add the chopped parsley.

BEEF PROVENCALE

Prep time: 2 5minutes

Total time: 6 hours 25 minutes

Serving: 5

Ingredients

- 3-lb. of beef chuck roast
- 2 tsp of kosher salt
- Freshly ground black pepper
- 3 tbsp of vegetable oil
- 1/3 cup of all-purpose flour

- 2 cups of chicken broth
- 14 1/2-oz. of whole peeled tomatoes, with their juice
- 1/4 cup of cognac or brandy
- 1 tbsp of herb
- 5 garlic cloves, peeled and smashed
- 4 medium carrots, peeled
- 1 fennel bulb, trimmed
- 1 onion, halved and thinly sliced
- 1/3 cup of prepared sun-dried tomato tapenade
- 1/3 cup of coarsely chopped fresh flat-leaf parsley
- 1 packed tsp of finely grated orange zest
- Hot buttered egg noodles, for serving

Directions

1. Prepare a medium-high flame with a big, heavy-bottomed pan. Add salt and pepper as need before cooking the meat. In a skillet, heat the oil until it begins to smoke. Sear the roast until it reveryes a deep mahogany color on both sides, which should take approximately 10 minutes. Stir the flour and roughly 1 1/2 cups of the chicken stock together in a medium bowl as the meat browns.
2. Toss the tomatoes and their juices into the slow cooker along with the herbes de Provence, the remaining 3 tbsp of of cognac, and the 2 tsp of salt.
3. Put the meat in the slow cooker once it has been browned. Scrape the browned pieces from the bottom of the pan with a wooden spoon after adding the remaining 1/2 cup of chicken stock to the skillet and letting it boil for a minute. Sprinkling the garlic, carrots, fennel, and onion over and around the meat after pouring the sauce over it. Sprinkle the flour mixture over the top. Put the lid on the slow cooker and cook on HIGH for 4 hours. Slow simmer the beef for up to 2 hours more over LOW heat until it is fork tender (for a total of 6

hours). The meat should be moved to a chopping board. Remove the fat off the surface of the cooking sauce.

4. The final step in the sauce is to: Mix in the remaining 1 tbsp of cognac along with the tomato tapenade, parsley, and orange zest to the slow cooker's veggies and sauce. As need, add salt and pepper. Cut the meat into thin slices and arrange them in a single row along the middle of a large serving plate. Put the meat in the center and the veggies around it, then cover everything with the sauce. Buttery egg noodles should be served hot with the dish. Get me the rest of the sauce please.

BEEF AND NOODLES

Prep time: 10 minutes

Total time: 35 minutes

Serving: 4

Ingredients

- 2 tbsp of vegetable oil
- 1 ¼ lbs. beef steak cut in bite size pieces
- 2 tbsp of butter
- 1 medium onion chopped
- 16 oz. of white button mushrooms halved
- 3 cloves garlic minced
- ½ tsp of marjoram
- ½ tsp of dried thyme leaves
- 8 oz. of egg noodles
- 2 ½ cups of low sodium beef broth
- 2 tsp of Worcestershire sauce
- 2 ½ tbsp of cornstarch
- Salt and pepper as need

- 1 tsp of chopped fresh parsley

Instructions

1. Bring oil for cooking to temperature in a large pot like a Dutch oven or cast iron pan. Beef should be browned on all sides. Take the steak out of the pan and serve it. Get under something to keep warm.
2. Butter should be melted in a pan over medium heat. Cook the onions and mushrooms for about 7 to 8 minutes, or until the onions are tender and the mushrooms are golden brown. Put the stove on low heat. Toss in the garlic, marjoram, and thyme and simmer for 1 minute, stirring constantly. Put the onions, mushrooms, and seasonings on a plate. Try to keep some body heat in by covering up.
3. Meanwhile, prepare the noodles as directed on the box and set aside to drain.
4. To the skillet, pour the beef broth and Worcestershire sauce. Raise the heat to a simmer and scrape the bottom of the pan to release any browned pieces. Whisk together the cornstarch and the 1/4 cup of cold water, then add to the pan. Reduce heat to low and cook, whisking regularly, until thickened.
5. Return the meat and mushroom combination to the pan and heat for two to three minutes. Salt & pepper as need. Sprinkle some freshly cut parsley over cooked egg noodles and serve.

CHEESY RAMEN NOODLES

Prep time: 5 minutes

Total time: 5 minutes

Serving: 1

Ingredients

- 2 cups of water
- 3-oz. of package any flavor ramen noodles
- 1 slice American cheese

Directions

1. Start a pot of water boiling. Add the ramen noodles and simmer for 2 minutes, or until they are soft. After discarding the water, mix in the spice package and the cheese until everything is evenly distributed.

BEEF BROCCOLI AND PORTOBELLO PASTA

Prep time: 15 minutes

Total time: 55 minutes

Serving: 4

Ingredients

- 500 g fettuccine
- 750 g beef steaks
- 1 head broccoli, cut into florets
- 6 pcs Portobello mushrooms, sliced
- 200 ml cream
- 1/2 cup of grated parmesan cheese
- 1/3 cup of dry white wine

- 2 cups of beef stock
- 1 tsp of dried thyme
- 1 white onion, chopped
- 4 cloves garlic, minced
- 2 tbsp of butter
- salt
- freshly ground black pepper
- olive oil

Instructions

1. Prepare broccoli by blanching the florets in boiling water for 90 seconds, then draining and rinsing under cold water. Put aside for a moment.
2. Salt and pepper the beef steaks, then sear them in a heavy skillet for three minutes per side. After the steaks have rested for 10 minutes, slice them against the grain.
3. Prepare fettuccine according to package directions, but cook it for two minutes less. Drain and leave aside.
4. Cut the steak across the grain into very thin slices. Conserve the fluids.
5. Onions and garlic should be sautéed in a big pan with melted butter over low heat until the onions are translucent and the garlic has softened, about a minute.
6. Fry the mushrooms in in olive oil until they start to turn brown around the edges.
7. Simmer for 2 minutes after adding the wine and the saved beef liquid.
8. The stock is poured in, brought to a boil, the parmesan cheese is added, and the sauce is allowed to simmer to thicken somewhat.
9. Mix in the chopped meat, broccoli, and pasta, then pour in the cream and stir again. Preparation time: 2 minutes.
10. Add some salt and freshly ground pepper before serving.

PICNIC SALAD RECIPES

Prep time: 15 minutes

Total time: 1 hours 15 minutes

Serving: 8

Ingredients

- 6 Cups of Broccoli Florets Chopped
- 1/4 Cup of Red Onions Thinly Sliced
- 1/2 Cup of Cooked Bacon Chopped
- 1/2 Cup of Dried Cranberries
- 1/4 Cup of Sunflower Seeds Shelled
- 1/2 Cup of Shredded Sharp Cheddar Cheese
- 1 Cup of Mayo
- 3 Tbsp of Sugar
- 2 Tbsp of Cider Vinegar
- Salt and Pepper as need

Instructions

1. Broccoli, onion, sunflower seeds, bacon, cranberries, and cheddar cheese should all be mixed together in a big bowl.
2. Mix the mayonnaise, sugar, vinegar, salt, and pepper together in a small bowl.
3. Toss the broccoli mixture well with the dressing.
4. After chilling for an hour, toss again before serving.

VEGETABLE RAMEN

Prep time:30 minutes

Total time: 40 minutes

Serving:4

Ingredients

- 2 packages instant noodles
- 1 tbsp of soy sauce
- 1 tsp of dark soy sauce
- 1 tsp of vegetarian oyster sauce
- ½ tsp of sugar
- ½ tsp of sesame oil
- Fresh ground white pepper
- 2 tbsp of canola oil
- 2 cloves garlic (sliced)
- ¼ cup of sweet red bell peppers or Holland chilies
- 5 fresh shiitake mushrooms
- 1 medium carrot
- 1 ½ cups of cabbage
- 1 tbsp of Shaoxing wine
- 1 cup of snow peas
- 1 cup of fresh mung bean sprouts
- 2 scallions

Instructions

1. Remove the flavor packet from the instant ramen and throw it away. Prepare a pot of boiling water that can hold 6 cups of. Noodles should be added and cooked for 45 seconds to 1 minute, while being stirred regularly using chopsticks or a fork. Rehydrating the ramen is all that's required to make it lose its square shape and become more appetizing. It's crucial at this stage that the ramen not be overcooked. Drain

the ramen in a strainer as soon as it is rehydrated, then rinse them under cold water to end the cooking process and get rid of the extra starch.

2. Whisk together the two types of soy sauce, the oyster sauce, the sugar, the sesame oil, and the white pepper. Start by putting the oil and garlic in the wok and heating it up over high heat. Peppers, mushrooms, carrots, and cabbage should be added right away and stir-fried for a full minute. After that, pour in the Shaoxing wine and keep cooking for another 15 seconds.

3. Then, add the cooked noodles, breaking them up if they're clumped. Coat the noodles thoroughly with the soy sauce mixture. Use a scooping motion to stir-fry for about 20 seconds, or until the sauce is evenly dispersed. Blend in the bean sprouts, onions, and snow peas. Stir for a another minute, and then serve.

TOFU RAMEN

Prep time:5 minutes

Total time: 45 minutes

Serving:4

Ingredients

- 12 to 16 oz. of extra-firm tofu
- 2 tbsp of toasted sesame oil, divided
- 2 tbsp of olive oil, divided
- 6 tbsp of white miso paste, divided
- 2 tbsp of soy sauce, divided
- 1 cup of sweet yellow onion, sliced
- 8 oz. of baby bella mushrooms
- 1 cup of Napa cabbage, thinly sliced

- 3 green onions
- 4 garlic cloves
- 2 large carrots
- 8 oz. of dry ramen noodles
- 4 cups of vegetable broth
- 1 tbsp of mirin
- ¼ cup of coconut milk
- 2 cups of spinach leaves
- Sesame seeds, for garnish

Instructions

1. Drain the tofu after removing it from the packaging. Tofu should be cut in half lengthwise and placed in a deep basin. For best results, remove liquid by microwaving on high for 2 minutes. Remove any moisture that was produced when microwaving. A towel, a cutting board, and something heavy should be used to press the two parts together. Press for 15 minutes, or until all water has been extracted.
2. Cut the onion in half. The mushrooms should be cut into slices. Slice the cabbage very thinly. Green onions should be sliced very thinly. Sliver the garlic cloves as thinly as possible. Matchstick-size pieces of carrot.
3. Cube the tofu so that it is easily digestible. One tbsp of toasted sesame oil and one tbsp of olive oil should be heated over medium heat. Toss in the tofu and cook for approximately 10 minutes, stirring periodically, until browned and crisp. In the meantime, mix 2 tbsp of. miso, 1 tbsp of. soy sauce, and 1 tbsp of. After the tofu has browned, remove it from the stove and, working quickly, pour the sauce over it, being careful not to burn yourself. For an extra aromatic minute of cooking time over medium heat, stir sauce into tofu.
4. Bring a large saucepan of water to a boil, then add the noodles and simmer until they are firm to the bite. Retain the liquid, but put the draining water aside. If the noodles have

gotten cold while waiting to be served, run them under hot water.

5. Prepare the stock by: One tbsp of sesame oil and one tbsp of olive oil should be heated over medium heat in a big saucepan or Dutch oven. After 4 minutes, add the onion and cook until it begins to brown. Put in the garlic and heat for 30 seconds, stirring regularly, until it begins to turn brown. Bring the vegetable broth to a low boil and add it.

6. After around 10 minutes of cooking time, add the mushrooms, carrots, mirin, and 3 tbsp of miso paste. Stir in the remaining 1 tbsp of soy sauce along with the coconut milk, green onions, cabbage, and spinach. Cook until the spinach has wilted, about 1 minute. Add extra miso paste as need, up to another tbsp of.

7. Distribute the noodles among four serving dishes. Layer the tofu, veggies, and broth on the rice. Separate containers for the broth and noodles can be used to store any leftovers.

SHIO RAMEN RECIPE

Prep time:20 minutes

Total time: 8 hours 20 minutes

Serving:4

Ingredients

For the Dashi:

- 1/4 oz. of kombu, or dried kelp
- 1/4 oz. of dried shiitake mushroom
- 1 oz. of shaved katsuobushi flakes

For the Shio Ramen:

- 2 quarts chintan chicken stock

- 1/2 cup of shio tare
- 4 servings ramen noodles
- 1/2 cup of aromatic oil, schmaltz
- Toppings, such as chashu
- 2 scallions, sliced as thinly as possible

Directions

1. Refrigerate the kombu and shiitake mushroom mixture for at least 8 and up to 24 hours in a sealed container.
2. Over medium heat, put the kombu and shiitake mushrooms in a small saucepan with the water. Don't let the water boil, since doing so will make the kombu bitter and ruin the dashi. Bring to a minimal simmer and turn off the heat. Put in the katsuobushi and let it sit for three minutes. Get a heat-safe bowl and strain the dashi into it. The kombu, shiitakes, and katsuobushi can be used for something else, such niban dashi, or saved for later.
3. Image composite showing kombu being rehydrated after being extracted from dashi.
4. Raise the temperature of a large pot of water to a boil. Prepare dashi by adding it to chicken stock in a big pot and heating it over medium heat. To avoid cloudiness, do not allow the mixd broth to boil.
5. Start by heating water for the noodles, either using our homemade ramen noodle recipe or the directions on the box.
6. Pour 2 tsp of (30 ml) of shio tare into every of 4 preheated bowls. Fill every dish with about 1 1/2 cups of (350 ml) of the mixed broth. Examine the saltiness of the broth and adjust the seasonings accordingly. Every bowl can have extra broth or tare added as need.
7. The noodles should be drained and then divided into serving dishes. The noodles in the soup should have 1–2 tsp of (15–30 ml) of the fragrant oil drizzled over them. Sprinkle every bowl with the available toppings, such as chashu or

marinated eggs. Sprinkle some sliced scallions on top and serve right away.

SPICY VEGETARIAN RAMEN

Prep time:10 minutes

Total time: 30 minutes

Serving:2

Ingredients

- 2 TBSP OF light sesame oil or avocado oil
- 3/4-1 cup of chopped dried porcini mushrooms
- 3 cloves garlic, smashed and minced
- 4 scallions, thinly sliced white + greens
- 3-4 cups of low-sodium vegetable broth
- 2 tbsp of tomato paste
- 1-2 tbsp of Sriracha
- 1-2 tbsp of low-sodium soy sauce
- 4-5 oz. of uncooked ramen noodles

Fried garlic + chili oil

- 1/4 cup of avocado oil or vegetable oil
- 3 cloves garlic, thinly sliced
- 1 TBSP OF sesame seeds
- 1 TBSP OF crushed red chili flakes

Tasty topping options

- thinly sliced jalapeño
- edamame
- jammy soft-boiled egg
- chopped green onion and/or cilantro
- baby bok choy

- chili garlic sauce
- see blog post for even more topping ideas

Instructions

1. The fried garlic in chile oil comes first. On medium heat, prepare a quarter cup of oil in a medium saucepan. When the skillet is heated, add the sliced garlic and cook for about 3 minutes, turning often, until the garlic begins to turn golden. Once the garlic is toasted and crisp, add the sesame seeds and heat for another minute. Transfer the mixture to a small bowl and stir in the crushed red pepper. Mix and put away for later use.
2. Add a sprinkle of oil to the same saucepan and set it over medium heat before adding the garlic, green onion whites (keep the greens for topping), and dried porcini mushrooms. About a minute should be enough time to sauté until the food is aromatic.
3. Mix in the soy sauce, tomato paste, Sriracha, and broth.
4. Simmer, covered, on medium-low heat for 10 minutes.
5. While the soup is cooking, get the toppings ready.
6. When the broth is done and aromatic, strain it through a fine mesh screen or strainer to remove the onion and dried mushroom pieces before returning it to the saucepan.
7. Try some of the broth and adjust the seasonings as necessary. Sriracha may be used to increase the heat, while soy sauce can be used to increase the salty and umami. If you want your ramen more soupy, add another cup of broth and season as need.
8. Ramen noodles cooked in a pot of boiling water will take less time to soften than those cooked in a separate pot of water, but the resulting broth will be much thicker. Feel free to prepare the ramen separately and stir it into the soup right before serving if you like a lighter broth.

9. You may also add any additional vegetables you want cooked to the broth and let them soften there. Adjusting the flavor of this soup to your liking is a breeze.

PORK CHILI

Prep time:45 minutes

Total time: 2 hours 45 minutes

Serving:12

Ingredients

- 0-2 tbsp of vegetable oil, divided
- 1/2lb. of bacon
- 3-4 lb. of lean pork, trimmed and cut into bite sized pieces
- 1 onion, chopped
- 2 fresh or frozen jalapeño peppers, seeded and minces
- 3 red bell peppers, seeded and chopped
- 4 large garlic cloves, minced
- 2 tsp of dried oregano
- 1 Tbsp of chili powder
- 1 Tbsp of ground cumin
- 1/4 tsp of cayenne
- 4 cups of beef broth
- 1 28-oz. of can crushed tomatoes
- 2 10-oz. of cans fire roasted tomatoes with chilis
- 3 15-oz. of cans of beans, drained and rinsed

Instructions

1. The bacon should be cooked until it's crispy in a large stockpot. Pull out and set aside, then discard all except 2 tbsp of the fat from the cooking kettle. Shake up the bacon.

2. Season the pork chunks with salt & pepper and pat them dry. If the pot needs more oil, add some now. It's best to brown the pork in stages and then move it to a separate dish using a slotted spoon.
3. The onion should be added and cooked, turning occasionally, until it is tender. Cook for one more minute after adding the garlic and seasonings. Bring the drippings back into the saucepan and add the bacon and pork. To the broth, chilies, bell peppers, tomatoes with chilies, and tomato purée, bring to a boil.
4. Cover and simmer the chili for 1-1 1/2 hours, stirring periodically, or until the meat is fork tender. Beans should be added and cooked for another half hour after being stirred in.
5. The best way to eat chili is with all the fixings.

LAKSA INSTANT RAMEN

Prep time:10 minutes

Total time:10 minutes

Serving:2

Ingredients

- 3 tbsp of laksa paste
- 2 tsp of brown sugar
- 3 1/2 cups of water
- 1 cup of coconut milk
- 1 package Maruchan Chicken-flavored Instant Noodles
- 1 package Maruchan Shrimp flavored Instant Noodles
- 1/4 cup of cilantro leaves
- 1 scallion
- 1 Thai bird chili
- 2 lime wedges

Instructions

1. Over medium heat, put a medium-sized saucepan. Stirring constantly, boil the laksa paste and brown sugar for 1 minute.
2. Put in the instant noodle flavoring packages, water, and coconut milk. Get it to a low boil.
3. Just 2 minutes of cooking time should be enough to soften the instant noodles while keeping them al dente.
4. Split the noodles and soup in half and serve every half with a handful of cilantro, a few scallions, a pinch of chili powder (if using), and a slice of lime. Dish up right away.

CREAMY VEGAN RAMEN

Prep time:10 minutes

Total time: 30 minutes

Serving: 4

Ingredients

- 1 tbsp of vegetable oil
- 1 small onion, diced
- 2 tsp of fresh ginger, grated
- 2 tsp of garlic, minced
- 1 medium carrot, shredded
- 6 cups of hot water
- ¼ cup of miso paste
- 2 tbsp of smooth peanut butter
- 2 cups of fresh shiitake mushrooms
- 3 packs dried ramen noodles
- 1 tbsp of green onions, finely chopped
- ¼ tsp of ground black pepper
- For serving:

- ¼ cup of shelled edamame beans, cooked
- ¼ cup of frozen sweet corn, thawed
- ¼ cup of carrot, shredded
- 2 tbsp of green onions, finely chopped
- 1 tbsp of sesame seeds

Instructions

1. Put oil in a Dutch oven that holds 5.5 quarts and heat it for 1 minute over medium heat, or until it begins to sizzle. Sauté the onion, ginger, and garlic for about a minute, or until soft and aromatic.
2. Carrot should be added and cooked for about 2 minutes, stirring occasionally.
3. Pour the boiling water in gradually (or stock). Simmer for 3–4 minutes while stirring periodically.
4. Two minutes should be enough time to dissolve the miso paste and peanut butter in a pot with a stir.
5. For approximately 4 minutes, if you add mushrooms to a pan and cook them over medium heat, they will become soft.
6. Put the ramen noodles in the miso soup and simmer for 2 to 3 minutes, or until they are soft as directed on the package. If you want to avoid the noodles sticking together, you should stir them often using chopsticks or a fork.
7. Cook until green onions are tender, then add black pepper if you want it spicy. Put the saucepan aside and turn off the stove.
8. You may drain the noodles using a steel mesh strainer or a slotted spoon before placing them in bowls for your guests. Put the broth and mushrooms over the noodles gradually with a soup ladle. Sprinkle with a few edamame, maize, shredded carrot, and sliced green onion spoonfuls.
9. Serve right away with a sprinkle of sesame seeds.

QUICK AND EASY VEGAN RAMEN

Prep time:5 minutes

Total time: 20 minutes

Serving: 4

Ingredients

- 2 tbsp of avocado oil
- 4 green onion, chopped into 1-inch pieces
- 4 garlic cloves, cut in halves
- 3-inch cube of ginger, cut into 4 pieces
- 1 oz dried shitake mushrooms
- 1-litre vegetable broth
- 1 cup of water
- 2 tbsp of soy sauce
- 1 tbsp of miso paste
- 1 tsp of agave
- 1 block soft tofu, cut into small cubes
- 2 packs vegan ramen noodles
- spinach, cilantro, & green onions to garnish

Instructions

1. For medium-high heat, bring a big pot of avocado oil to the table.
2. The green onion, garlic, and ginger need to be sautéed for 2 minutes after being added to the saucepan.
3. Toss in some dried shiitakes and continue cooking for another 2 minutes.
4. Cook for 10 minutes, covered, over low heat, after adding the vegetable broth, water, soy sauce, miso paste, and agave and bringing to a boil.

5. You may (optionally) filter the soup to get rid of the large pieces of garlic and ginger, or you can use a fork to fish them out.
6. Turn the heat up to medium and add the tofu and ramen noodles. Cook for 2–3 minutes, or until the noodles are soft.
7. Baby spinach, sliced green onion, and chopped fresh cilantro are great additions.

10 MINUTE SPINACH RAMEN

Prep time:5 minutes

Total time: 10 minutes

Serving:1

Ingredients

- 1 portion of ramen or egg noodles
- 1.5 cups of vegetable broth or stock
- 1 Tbsp of soy sauce
- ¼ tsp of toasted sesame oil
- ½ red chili, sliced
- 2 handfuls fresh baby spinach
- 1 egg
- Ground black pepper, as need

Instructions

1. Put the ramen in the microwave. Make sure the noodles are fully cooked by simmering them in the liquid.
2. In the meantime, use another stovetop to cook or poach your egg.
3. After the ramen has finished cooking, throw in some greens. Just before the noodles are done, add the frozen spinach and crank the heat back up to a simmer as quickly as possible;

the spinach will defrost and separate, and the dish will be ready to serve. Fresh spinach should be added after the noodles are done cooking, and the heat turned off; the spinach should be stirred in until it has wilted.

4. Toss with some soy sauce, sesame oil, and freshly ground black pepper.
5. Top the ramen with the egg, chile, some more pepper, and toasted sesame oil.

PORK & SHRIMP WONTON SOUP

Prep time:15 minutes

Total time: 30 minutes

Serving:3

Ingredients

For the wontons

- ¾ lb. of ground pork
- ½ lb. of peeled and deveined shrimp finely chopped
- 4 green onions thinly sliced
- 1 tbsp of soy sauce
- 1 tsp of toasted sesame oil
- 1 tsp of minced fresh ginger
- 1 small garlic clove minced
- 1 tsp of cornstarch
- ½ tsp of kosher salt
- ¼ tsp of ground white pepper
- 12- oz. of package square wonton wrappers

For the soup

- 6 cups of chicken broth

- 1 tbsp of minced ginger
- 2 tbsp of soy sauce
- 1 tbsp of Shiaoxing wine
- 1 tbsp of sesame oil
- 4 to 6 leaves bok choy
- ½ lb. of shrimp peeled and deveined
- 3 scallions thinly sliced

Instructions

1. The wontons are prepared by Mix the pork, shrimp, green onions, soy sauce, sesame oil, ginger, garlic, cornstarch, salt, and pepper together in a large bowl.
2. Brush the edges of two adjacent sides of a wonton wrapper with water, then fill the middle with approximately a tsp of of the filling. Make a triangle out of the wrapper by folding over one corner so that the wet sides meet the dry sides. For a secure closure, please press the sides together. Then, using your hands, draw the corners of the long side of the triangle together to make a handbag. A little water will do the trick for gluing the edges together. Spread the remaining filling and wrappers out on a parchment-lined baking sheet and repeat with the rest.
3. The soup is prepared by simmering chicken broth, ginger, soy sauce, cooking wine, and sesame oil in a medium pot over high heat.
4. Simmer for around 10 minutes with the lid on and the heat at medium. After the stock has come to a boil, add the bok choy, shrimp, and green onions and simmer until the shrimp are pink and opaque throughout, about 2 minutes.
5. Meanwhile, start boiling a big pot of water. Cook the wontons (in batches if necessary) for about 5 minutes, or until they float to the surface. Prepare three to five wontons for every person. I normally make 16 servings for 4, but you may need more depending on the appetites of your guests.

6. Split the prawns and bok choy amongst 4 bowls using a slotted spoon. The next step is to serve wontons in individual bowls.
7. Ladle the soup stock over the shrimp, wontons, and bok choy before serving.
8. Dish up right away.

EASY SPICY SHOYU RAMEN

Prep time:10 minutes

Total time: 30 minutes

Serving:2

Ingredients

- 1 TBSP OF sesame oil, more if necessary
- 3 cloves of garlic, grated to a paste or finely minced
- 1 TBSP OF grated fresh ginger
- 1 cup of sliced shiitake mushrooms
- 1 TBSP OF spicy chili bean paste
- 3 TBSP OF low sodium soy sauce
- 1/2 TBSP OF rice wine vinegar
- 1 tsp of sea salt
- 1 tsp of sugar
- 2 cups of chicken stock
- 2 cups of dashi stock

Toppings:

- Soft-boiled egg
- Sliced scallions
- Narutomaki
- Protein of choice
- Julienned carrots

- Sesame seeds
- Pinch of white pepper
- 2 packets of uncooked Ramen noodles

Instructions

1. In a large saucepan, melt the sesame oil over a moderate flame. The garlic and ginger should be added to the boiling oil and allowed to simmer for about 30 seconds while being stirred frequently.
2. Put in the shiitake mushrooms and cook for two to three minutes, or until they're softened.
3. Stir the chile paste around until the mushrooms are evenly covered.
4. Put in the sugar, salt, rice vinegar, and soy sauce. Swirl in the chicken and dashi stock and give it another stir.
5. Soup should be simmered for at least 15 minutes. While it's simmering, you can cook the ramen noodles, the egg, and the other ingredients.
6. After simmering for 15 minutes, taste the soup and add more chili pepper flakes or soy sauce to make it more to your liking.
7. When the noodles are cooked, drain them and place them in a big bowl. After placing noodles in a dish, pour broth over them and sprinkle with toppings of your choice.

VEGAN SHOYU RAMEN

Prep time:20 minutes

Total time: 1 hours 30 minutes

Serving:3

Ingredients

- 4 oz of firm tofu pressed
- 3-4 servings of ramen noodles used fresh ramen
- Menma seasoned bamboo shoots
- A handful of chopped scallions
- cooking oil

Broth

- 4 slices of ginger
- 10 dried Shiitake mushrooms cleaned
- 1 cup of raw cashew
- 3 leeks chopped
- 1.5 lbs daikon radish
- 2 small garlic bulbs cut in half
- 1 oz kombu
- 20 cups of of water
- ½ tsp of salt
- 1 tsp of mushrooms seasoning

Tare

- 1 cup of light soy sauce
- ½ cup of dark soy sauce
- ⅓ cup of sake
- ⅓ cup of mirin
- 2-3 stalks scallion white part only
- 2-3 garlic cloves mashed
- 3 slices of ginger

Instructions

Prepare the Broth

1. In a large stockpot, sauté the ginger and mushrooms in a tbsp of oil until fragrant. The cashews, leek, and daikon radish should be stir-fried for a few more minutes. Cook the water

on high heat. Put the kombu and garlic bulb into the water and sprinkle the salt over the top.

2. Bring the saucepan to a boil with the cover on, and then reduce the heat to low and simmer for 45 minutes. After the soup has come to a boil, skim off the scum and discard the kombu. Using a mushroom seasoning is a great idea.

Prepare the Tare and Tofu

1. Put everything for the tare into a small pot and heat to a full boil. Reduce heat to low and simmer, uncovered, for 10 to 15 minutes, or until reduced by half. I like to let the aromatics steep in the tare for as long as possible to get the most flavor out of it, so put it aside. After it has cooled, put it in a jar to use at a later time if you don't plan on using it right away.
2. Divide the tofu into quarters and arrange it in a single layer on a wide platter. Marinate for at least 15 minutes in a serving (approximately 2 tbsp of) of tare.
3. The next step is to heat a pan that won't stick and add a little oil. Prepare the tofu by pan-frying it for 2–3 minutes on every side over medium heat, or until a thin crust develops. Do not cut into it until it has cooled fully.

How to serve

1. Now transfer the soup to a second pot and remove the mushrooms and kelp (if they weren't already). The broth should be kept heated over low heat.
2. Mung bean sprouts need only a quick blanch in boiling water (for a few seconds). Cook the ramen noodles according to the package instructions using the same pot.
3. To serve, place 2 tsp of tare (the exact amount can be modified to suit your palate) in a bowl and pour the broth on top. Noodles, mung bean sprouts, menma, sliced scallions, and tofu cha shu can be added to the dish. Serve hot.

SPICY CHEESE RAMEN RECIPE

Prep time:5 minutes

Total time:5 minutes

Serving:1

Ingredients

- 1 pack Samyang instant noodles
- 1 cup of milk
- 2 cups of water
- grated or sliced cheese
- green onions garnish

Instructions

1. Instant noodles should be cooked by bringing water to a boil and then adding them. Toss and stir for a just minute or two.
2. Drain the saucepan's water and replace it with milk.
3. Once the milk begins to boil, sprinkle in the instant noodle flavoring. Make sure to stir it for a full minute.
4. Turn off the heat when the soup bubbles and sprinkle cheese over the ramen.
5. Green onions can be added as a finishing touch once the cheese has melted.

TOMATO RAMEN

Prep time:20 minutes

Total time:40 minutes

Serving:2

Ingredients

- 300 g Ramen
- 100 g Chicken Breast
- 80 g Spinach
- 200 g Canned Diced Tomatoes
- 100 ml Water
- 100 ml Soy Milk
- 15 g Chinese Chicken Broth
- 15 g Olive Oil
- Black Pepper As need
- Basil As need
- 5 g Powder Cheese As need

Instructions

Soup

1. Make bite-sized chunks of the chicken and spinach.
2. Put the crushed tomatoes, water, chicken broth, and basil in a saucepan and bring to a boil.
3. Throw in some soy milk.

Toppings

1. Saute the chicken breast in the olive oil in a frying pan. Cook the chicken well and season with black pepper as need.
2. The same method of cooking should be used for the spinach.
3. While that's going on, you can get the ramen boiling in a different pot of water.

4. After the noodles have finished cooking, pour the soup into bowls. The ramen should be put in last, taking care that the noodles don't become twisted.
5. Then, when everything else has been added, sprinkle on the powdered cheese.

SESAME-GINGER CUCUMBER SOBA NOODLE SALAD

Prep time:10 minutes

Total time:16 minutes

Serving:3

Ingredients

- 1 package soba noodles
- 1 large English cucumber, julienned
- 1/2 cup of cilantro, roughly chopped
- lime wedges

Ginger Scallion Sauce

- 3/4 cup of scallions thinly sliced
- 2 cloves garlic, minced
- 2 tbsp of fresh ginger, grated or minced
- 2 tbsp of sesame seeds
- 3 tbsp of rice wine vinegar
- 2 tbsp of pure maple syrup
- 1 tbsp of toasted sesame oil
- 2 tbsp of tamari, soy sauce or Namo Shoyu
- 2 tsp of red pepper flakes, as need
- 1/2 tsp of sriracha, optional

Instructions

1. Mix the sauce ingredients in a small dish and put aside.
2. You should prepare soba noodles in accordance with the package's instructions. If you're using 100% buckwheat noodles, I think the flavor might benefit from a generous amount of salt added to the cooking water (something I wouldn't normally recommend). Once the soba noodles have finished boiling, they should be rinsed under cold running water to stop the cooking process and prevent them from becoming mushy.
3. Use a julienne peeler to cut your cucumber into thin strips as you wait. You can choose to halve your cucumber lengthwise before julienne-cutting it if it is very lengthy. Those who own a spiralizer can also spiralize. If you don't have a julienne tool, you may always just chop them into thin strips about 1/4 inch wide and 1 1/2 inches long.
4. After rinsing the noodles, put them back into the same pot they were cooked in with the cucumber, cilantro, and roughly three quarters of the sauce.
5. To serve, place half of the noodle mixture in a single serving dish, cover with half of the remaining sauce, and season with salt and pepper as need. Juice from as many limes as you desire. The lime was my favorite part, and I probably ate the equivalent of two ripe ones just for myself.
6. Prepare hot or cold.

EASY REAL TONKOTSU RAMEN

Prep time: 5 minutes

Total time: 20 minutes

Serving:4

Ingredients

- 3 to 4 oz pork fat
- 2 cups of chicken stock
- 2 cups of dashi stock
- 2 cups of unsweetened soy milk

For a Bowl of Ramen

- 1 portion fresh frozen or instant ramen noodles
- 3 to 4 tbsp of tsuyu chashu tare
- 1 green onion, chopped
- Handful beansprouts
- Handful black fungus
- 1 to 2 slices of chashu
- 1/2 to 1 ramen egg
- 1 clove garlic, optional

Instructions

1. Throw some pork fat into a medium saucepan and fill it with water until the pig is submerged. Bring it to a boil over medium-high heat and cook the pork belly for 5–7 minutes, or until it reveryes an internal temperature of 165°F. Remove the pig fat off the rind and chop it into tiny pieces. Blend the chicken stock in at high speed for about 2 minutes, or until smooth. Add the dashi stock and unsweetened soy milk to the pork fat and chicken stock mixture that you just poured out of the now-clean saucepan. Over medium heat, stir the mixture and bring it to a simmer. In addition, you

should put another pot of water on to boil for the noodles and extras.

2. In the meantime, let's get the ramen toppings ready. Prepare a green onion salad by dicing green onions. Make long, thin strips out of the black fungus. Chashu has to be seared for 3–5 minutes on a dry pan over high heat, torch, or high broil.

3. To blanch bean sprouts, place them in a pot of boiling water for one minute. Drain well, then put aside. The next step is to blanch the black fungus for 1 minute before taking it out of the water. Do a thorough draining, and then set away. It's time to get the noodle pot going. It will only take 2 minutes, whether you use a fresh or frozen option. A bowl of instant ramen noodles will be ready in three to four minutes.

4. Add tsuyu or chashu tare to a serving dish while the noodles boil. Carefully add 1 1/2 cups of of the broth we produced earlier. Mix in a harmonious fashion. Put the drained, cooked noodles in a bowl. Toss noodles in a large bowl and stir in enough liquid to cover. Put the ramen egg, chashu, bean sprouts, black fungus, and green onions on top of the noodles. Garlic cloves can be grated in at the end for added flavor. This rich, thick soup will benefit greatly from the addition of this pungent, spicy garlic. Enjoy!

SHIITAKE KOMBU DASHI

Prep time: 5 minutes

Total time: 5 minutes

Serving:1

Ingredients

- 10 g Dried Shiitake Mushrooms
- 10 g Kombu
- 800 ml Water

Instructions

1. Fill a glass jar with water and add shiitake mushrooms and kombu.
2. Don't remove the jar from the refrigerator for at least 5 hours.
3. Take out the shiitake and kombu when the soup reveryes a golden-brown color and use it as dashi.

SOY SAUCE SEASONING

Prep time: 30 minutes

Total time: 35 minutes

Serving:10

Ingredients

- 1 oz. of dried fish anchovy, bonito
- 1 oz. of dried shiitake mushroom
- 1¾ cups of water
- 2 oz. of konbu
- Salt
- 2 cups of dark soy sauce

Instructions

1. Prepare the powder by grinding the dried fish and shiitake mushrooms in a spice grinder.
2. Soak the konbu in the water and pour the mixture into a large stockpot. Toss it in the microwave and microwave it until it boils. Remove the konbu after 2 minutes of simmering and toss it.
3. Fish and mushroom powder should be added to the water that is already simmering and brought back to a boil. Turn off the heat when the liquid boils, then drain it through a paper or cloth filter (a coffee filter works well for this).
4. If you'd rather use a liquid measure, you can do so by weighing the salt in the container. Prepare by salting.
5. You may also just add a third of a cup of and a tsp of of salt to 2 cups of of the liquid. The amount of tare you end up with will be lower since you will waste some of the liquid you produce.
6. Coat everything in salt and stir it in.

7. The liquid and salt combination should be poured from a measuring cup of into a big bowl. Soy sauce of equal volume should be added to the bowl. Mix in a harmonious fashion.
8. If you store the tare in the fridge in an airtight container, it will keep for a few months.

Made in the USA
Las Vegas, NV
27 November 2024

12763429R00063